M68000

16/32-BIT MICROPROCESSOR
Programmer's Reference Manual

MOTOROLA

M68000

16/32-BIT MICROPROCESSOR
Programmer's Reference Manual

Fourth Edition

PRENTICE-HALL, Inc., Englewood Cliffs, N.J. 07632

Library of Congress Catalog Card No.: 83-62991

ISBN 0-13-566795-X
ISBN 0-13-541400-8 (Limited ed.)
ISBN 0-13-541392-3 (Special ed.)

Editorial/production supervision: Barbara A. Cassel
Manufacturing buyer: Gordon Osbourne

Printed in the United States of America

10 9 8 7 6 5 4 3

ISBN 0-13-566795-X
ISBN 0-13-541400-8 {LIMITED ED.}
ISBN 0-13-541392-3 {SPECIAL ED.}

Prentice-Hall International Inc., *London*
Prentice-Hall of Australia Pty. Limited, *Sydney*
Prentice-Hall do Brasil, Ltda., *Rio de Janiero*
Prentice-Hall Canada Inc., *Toronto*
Prentice-Hall of India Private Limited, *New Delhi*
Prentice-Hall of Japan, Inc., *Tokyo*
Prentice-Hall of Southeast Asia Pte. Ltd., *Singapore*
Whitehall Books Limited, *Wellington, New Zealand*

TABLE OF CONTENTS

Paragraph No. *Title* Page No.

Section 1
Architectural Description

1.1 Introduction 1
1.2 Programmer's Model 1
1.3 Software Development 6
1.3.1 Consistent Structure 6
1.3.2 Structured Modular Programming 6
1.3.3 Improved Software Testability 7
1.4 Virtual Memory/Machine Concepts 8
1.4.1 Virtual Memory 8
1.4.2 Virtual Machine...9
1.5 Reference Documentation..9

Section 2
Data Organization and Addressing Capabilities

2.1 Introduction 11
2.2 Operand Size 11
2.3 Data Organization in Registers 11
2.3.1 Data Registers 11
2.3.2 Address Registers 11
2.4 Data Organization in Memory 12
2.5 Addressing 13
2.6 Instruction Format 14
2.7 Program / Data References 15
2.8 Register Notation 15
2.9 Address Register Indirect Notation 15
2.10 Register Specification 16
2.11 Effective Address 16
2.11.1 Register Direct Modes 16
2.11.1.1 Data Register Direct 16
2.11.1.2 Address Register Direct 16
2.11.2 Memory Address Modes 17
2.11.2.1 Address Register Indirect 17
2.11.2.2 Address Register Indirect With Postincrement 17
2.11.2.3 Address Register Indirect With Predecrement 17
2.11.2.4 Address Register Indirect With Displacement 18
2.11.2.5 Address Register Indirect With Index 18
2.11.3 Special Address Modes 19
2.11.3.1 Absolute Short Address 19
2.11.3.2 Absolute Long Address 19
2.11.3.3 Program Counter With Displacement 20
2.11.3.4 Program Counter With Index 20
2.11.3.5 Immediate Data 21
2.11.4 Effective Address Encoding Summary 21
2.12 Implicit Reference 21
2.13 Stacks and Queues...22
2.12.1 System Stack 22
2.13.2 User Stacks 23
2.13.3 Queues 24

TABLE OF CONTENTS
(Continued)

Paragraph No.   *Title*   Page No.

Section 3
Instruction Set Summary

3.1	Introduction	27
3.2	Data Movement Operations	27
3.3	Integer Arithmetic Operations	27
3.4	Logical Operations	28
3.5	Shift and Rotate Operations	28
3.6	Bit Manipulation Operations	30
3.7	Binary Coded Decimal Operations	30
3.8	Program Control Operations	31
3.9	System Control Operations	32

Section 4
Exception Processing

4.1	Introduction	33
4.2	Privilege States	33
4.2.1	Supervisor State	34
4.2.2	User State	34
4.2.3	Privilege State Changes	35
4.2.4	Reference Classification	35
4.3	Exception Processing	35
4.3.1	Exception Vectors	35
4.3.2	Kinds of Exceptions	38
4.3.3	Multiple Exceptions	38
4.3.4	Exception Stack Frames	39
4.3.5	Exception Processing Sequence	40
4.4	Exception Processing Detailed Discussion	40
4.4.1	Reset	40
4.4.2	Interrupts	41
4.4.3	Uninitialized Interrupt	42
4.4.4	Spurious Interrupt	42
4.4.5	Instruction Traps	42
4.4.6	Illegal and Unimplemented Instructions	42
4.4.7	Privilege Violations	43
4.4.8	Tracing	43
4.4.9	Bus Error	44
4.4.9.1	Bus Error (MC68000/MC68008)	44
4.4.9.2	Bus Error (MC68010)	45
4.4.10	Address Error	47
4.5	Return From Exception (MC68010)	47

TABLE OF CONTENTS
(Continued)

Paragraph No.   *Title*   *Page No.*

Appendix A
Condition Codes Computation

A.1   Introduction 49
A.2   Condition Code Register 49
A.3   Condition Code Register Notation 49
A.4   Condition Code Computation 50
A.5   Conditional Tests 52

Appendix B
Instruction Set Details

B.1   Introduction 53
B.2   Addressing Categories 53
B.3   Instruction Description 54
B.4   Register Transfer Language Definitions 55

Appendix C
Instruction Format Summary

C.1   Introduction 165

Appendix D
MC68000 Instruction Execution Times

D.1   Introduction 187
D.2   Operand Effective Address Calculation Timing 187
D.3   Move Instruction Execution Times 188
D.4   Standard Instruction Execution Times 189
D.5   Immediate Instruction Execution Times 190
D.6   Single Operand Instruction Execution Times 191
D.7   Shift/Rotate Instruction Execution Times 191
D.8   Bit Manipulation Instruction Execution Times 192
D.9   Conditional Instruction Execution Times 192
D.10   JMP, JSR, LEA, PEA, and MOVEM Instruction Execution Times 193
D.11   Multi-Precision Instruction Execution Times 193
D.12   Miscellaneous Instruction Execution Times 194
D.13   Exception Processing Execution Times 195

TABLE OF CONTENTS
(Continued)

Paragraph No.   *Title*   *Page No.*

Appendix E
MC68008 Instruction Execution Times

E.1	Introduction	197
E.2	Operand Effective Address Calculation Times	197
E.3	Move Instruction Execution Times	198
E.4	Standard Instruction Execution Times	199
E.5	Immediate Instruction Execution Times	200
E.6	Single Operand Instruction Execution Times	201
E.7	Shift/Rotate Instruction Execution Times	201
E.8	Bit Manipulation Instruction Execution Times	202
E.9	Conditional Instruction Execution Times	202
E.10	JMP, JSR, LEA, PEA, and MOVEM Instruction Execution Times	203
E.11	Multi-Precision Instruction Execution Times	203
E.12	Miscellaneous Instruction Execution Times	204
E.13	Exception Processing Execution Times	205

Appendix F
MC68010 Instruction Execution Times

F.1	Introduction	207
F.2	Operand Effective Address Calculation Times	207
F.3	Move Instruction Execution Times	208
F.4	Standard Instruction Execution Times	209
F.5	Immediate Instruction Execution Times	210
F.6	Single Operand Instruction Execution Times	211
F.7	Shift/Rotate Instruction Execution Times	212
F.8	Bit Manipulation Instruction Execution Times	213
F.9	Conditional Instruction Execution Times	213
F.10	JMP, JSR, LEA, PEA, and MOVEM Instruction Execution Times	214
F.11	Multi-Precision Instruction Execution Times	214
F.12	Miscellaneous Instruction Execution Times	215
F.13	Exception Processing Execution Times	216

Appendix G
MC68010 Loop Mode Operation

G	MC68010 Loop Mode Operation	217

LIST OF ILLUSTRATIONS

Figure No.	Title	Page No.
1-1	User Programmer's Model (MC68000/MC68008/MC68010)	2
1-2	Supervisor Programmer's Model Supplement (MC68000/MC6808)	2
1-3	Supervisor Programmer's Model Supplement (MC68010)	3
1-4	Status Register	3
2-1	Word Organization In Memory	12
2-2	Data Organization In Memory	12
2-3	Memory Data Organization of the MC68008	14
2-4	Instruction Format	15
2-5	Single-Effective-Address-Instruction Operation Word — General Format	16
4-1	Exception Vector Format	36
4-2	Peripheral Vector Number Format	36
4-3	Address Translated from 8-Bit Vector Number (MC68000, MC68008)	36
4-4	Exception Vector Address Calculation (MC68010)	36
4-5	MC68000, MC68008 Group 1 and 2 Exception Stack Frame	39
4-6	MC68010 Stack Frame	39
4-7	Supervisor Stack Order for Bus or Address Error Exception	45
4-8	Exception Stack Order (Bus and Address Error)	46
4-9	Special Status Word Format	46
B-1	Instruction Description Format	54
G-1	DBcc Loop Program Example	217

LIST OF TABLES

Table No.	Title	Page No.
1-1	Data Addressing Modes	4
1-2	Instruction Set Summary	5
1-3	Variations of Instruction Types	5
2-1	Effective Address Encoding Summary	22
2-2	Implicit Instruction Reference Summary	22
3-1	Data Movement Operations	28
3-2	Integer Arithmetic Operations	29
3-3	Logical Operations	29
3-4	Shift and Rotate Operations	30
3-5	Bit Manipulation Operations	30
3-6	Binary Coded Decimal Operations	31
3-7	Program Control Operations	31
3-8	System Control Operations	32
4-1	Reference Classification	35
4-2	Exception Vector Assignment	37
4-3	Exception Grouping and Priority	38
4-4	MC68010 Format Codes	40
A-1	Condition Code Computations	51
A-2	Conditional Tests	52
B-1	Effective Addressing Mode Categories	53
C-1	Operation Code Map	165
C-2	Effective Address Encoding Summary	165
C-3	Conditional Tests	166
D-1	Effective Address Calculation Times	187
D-2	Move Byte and Word Instruction Execution Times	188
D-3	Move Long Instruction Execution Times	188
D-4	Standard Instruction Execution Times	189
D-5	Immediate Instruction Execution Times	190
D-6	Single Operand Instruction Execution Times	191
D-7	Shift/Rotate Instruction Execution Times	191
D-8	Bit Manipulation Instruction Execution Times	192
D-9	Conditional Instruction Execution Times	192
D-10	JMP, JSR, LEA, PEA, and MOVEM Instruction Execution Times	193
D-11	Multi-Precision Instruction Execution Times	193
D-12	Miscellaneous Instruction Execution Times	194
D-13	Move Peripheral Instruction Execution Times	194
D-14	Exception Processing Execution Times	195
E-1	Effective Address Calculation Times	197
E-2	Move Byte Instruction Execution Times	198
E-3	Move Word Instruction Execution Times	198

LIST OF TABLES
(Continued)

Paragraph No.	Title	Page No.
E-4	Move Long Instruction Execution Times	199
E-5	Standard Instruction Execution Times	199
E-6	Immediate Instruction Clock Periods	200
E-7	Single Operand Instruction Execution Times	201
E-8	Shift/Rotate Instruction Clock Periods	201
E-9	Bit Manipulation Instruction Execution Times	202
E-10	Conditional Instruction Execution Times	202
E-11	JMP, JSR, LEA, PEA, and MOVEM Instruction Execution Times	203
E-12	Multi-Precision Instruction Execution Times	203
E-13	Miscellaneous Instruction Execution Times	204
E-14	Move Peripheral Instruction Execution Times	204
E-15	Exception Processing Execution Times	205
F-1	Effective Address Calculation Times	207
F-2	Move Byte and Word Instruction Execution Times	208
F-3	Move Byte and Word Instruction Loop Mode Execution Times	208
F-4	Move Long Instruction Execution Times	208
F-5	Move Long Instruction Loop Mode Execution Times	209
F-6	Standard Instruction Execution Times	209
F-7	Standard Instruction Loop Mode Execution Times	210
F-8	Immediate Instruction Execution Times	210
F-9	Single Operand Instruction Execution Times	211
F-10	Clear Instruction Execution Times	211
F-11	Single Operand Instruction Loop Mode Execution Times	211
F-12	Shift/Rotate Instruction Execution Times	212
F-13	Shift/Rotate Instruction Loop Mode Execution Times	212
F-14	Bit Manipulation Instruction Execution Times	213
F-15	Conditional Instruction Execution Times	213
F-16	JMP, JSR, LEA, PEA, and MOVEM Instruction Execution Times	214
F-17	Multi-Precision Instruction Execution Times	214
F-18	Miscellaneous Instruction Execution Times	215
F-19	Exception Processing Execution Times	216
G-1	MC68010 Loopable Instructions	218

PREFACE

With the advent of 16-bit microprocessor technology, thorough, concise, and useful manuals must be provided to aid designers in development of their systems. This manual gives all the key information for software architects, computer designers, and programmers to complete software systems using Motorola's M68000 Family of Microprocessors. Hardware designers should consult the Advance Information data sheets for the appropriate microprocessor — MC68000, MC68008, and MC68010.

To facilitate design and for the fullest understanding, each instruction is described in detail in bit pattern format. Explicit examples are then shown to more thoroughly demonstrate how each instruction will operate.

This definitive information will allow the easiest and best designing possible. Additonally, the software in this manual will be upward compatible with all future M68000 family processors.

Information that is unique to the MC68010 is marked with a solid bar (▌) in the outside margin. Information that is unique to the MC68008 is marked with a dashed bar (▤).

M68000

16/32-BIT MICROPROCESSOR
Programmer's Reference Manual

SECTION 1
ARCHITECTURAL DESCRIPTION

1.1 INTRODUCTION

In 1979, Motorola introduced the first implementation of the M68000 16/32-bit microprocessor architecture — the MC68000. The MC68000, with a 16-bit data bus and 24-bit address bus, was only the first in a family of processors which implement a comprehensive, extensible computer architecture. It was soon followed by the MC68008, with an 8-bit data bus and 20-bit address bus, and by the MC68010, which introduced the virtual machine aspects of the M68000 architecture. Soon the MC68020 with its 32-bit data and address buses will be introduced, implementing the next stage of the M68000.

This manual is intended to serve as a programmer's reference for both systems and applications programmers of the three current implementations of the M68000 — the MC68008, the MC68000, and the MC68010. The hardware system design aspects of these processors, such as bus structure and control, are presented in the respective advance information data sheets for each device.

The MC68000 and the MC68008 are identical from the view of the programmer, with the exception that the MC68000 can directly access 16 megabytes (24 bits of address) and the MC68008 can directly access 1 megabyte (20 bits of address). The MC68010 has much in common with the first two devices but also possesses some additional instructions and registers as well as full virtual machine/memory capability. Since the processors are so similar to the programmer, only the differences are highlighted. When the M68000 is referenced, the feature described is common to all. If a particular feature is applicable only to one processor, the MC part number will be referenced.

1.2 PROGRAMMER'S MODEL

The M68000 executes instructions in one of two modes — user mode or supervisor mode. The user mode is intended to provide the execution environment for the majority of application programs. The supervisor mode allows some additional instructions and privileges and is intended for use by the operating system and other system software. See **SECTION 4 EXCEPTION PROCESSING** for further details.

To provide for the upward compatibility of code written for a specific implementation of the M68000, the user programmer's model is common to all implementations. The user programmer's model is shown in Figure 1-1

As shown in the user programmer's model, the M68000 offers 16 32-bit general purpose registers (D0-D7, A0-A7), a 32-bit program counter, and an 8-bit condition code register. The first eight registers (D0-D7) are used as data registers for byte (8-bit), word (16-bit),

1

and long word (32-bit) operations. The second set of seven registers (A0-A6) and the stack pointer (USP) may be used as software stack pointers and base address registers. In addition, the address registers may be used for word and long word operations. All of the 16 registers may be used as index registers.

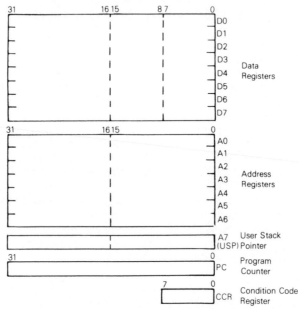

Figure 1-1. User Programmer's Model (MC68000/MC68008/MC68010)

The supervisor programmer's model includes some supplementary registers in addition to the above mentioned registers. The MC68000 and the MC68008 contain identical supervisor mode register resources. These are shown in Figure 1-2 and include the status register (high order byte) and the supervisor stack pointer (A7′).

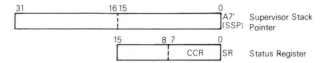

Figure 1-2. Supervisor Programmer's Model Supplement (MC68000/MC68008)

The supervisor programming model supplement of the MC68010 is shown in Figure 1-3. In addition to the supervisor stack pointer and status register, it includes the vector base register and the alternate function code registers.

The vector base register is used to determine the location of the exception vector table in memory to support multiple vector tables. The alternate function code registers allow the supervisor to access user data space or emulate CPU space cycles.

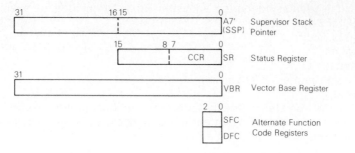

Figure 1-3. Supervisor Programmer's Model Supplement (MC68010)

The status register, shown in Figure 1-4, contains the interrupt mask (eight levels available) as well as the condition codes: overflow (V), zero (Z), negative (N), carry (C), and extend (X). Additional status bits indicate that the processor is in a trace (T) mode and/or in a supervisor (S) state.

Five basic data types are supported. These data types are:
- Bits
- BCD Digits (4 Bits)
- Bytes (8 Bits)
- Words (16 Bits)
- Long Words (32 Bits)

In addition, operations on other data types such as memory addresses, status word data, etc. are provided for in the instruction set.

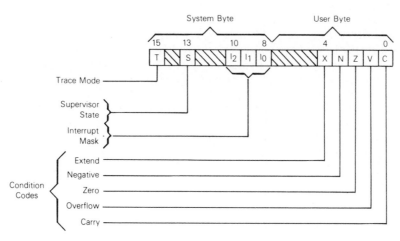

Figure 1-4. Status Register

The 14 flexible addressing modes, shown in Table 1-1, include six basic types:
- Register Direct
- Register Indirect
- Absolute
- Immediate
- Program Counter Relative
- Implied

Included in the register indirect addressing modes is the capability to do post-incrementing, predecrementing, offsetting, and indexing. Program counter relative mode can also be modified via indexing and offsetting.

Table 1-1. Data Addressing Modes

Mode	Generation
Register Direct Addressing	
Data Register Direct	EA = Dn
Address Register Direct	EA = An
Absolute Data Addressing	
Absolute Short	EA = (Next Word)
Absolute Long	EA = (Next Two Words)
Program Counter Relative Addressing	
Relative with Offset	EA = (PC) + d_{16}
Relative with Index and Offset	EA = (PC) + (Xn) + d_8
Register Indirect Addressing	
Register Indirect	EA = (An)
Postincrement Register Indirect	EA = (An), An ← An + N
Predecrement Register Indirect	An ← An − N, EA = (An)
Register Indirect with Offset	EA = (An) + d_{16}
Indexed Register Indirect with Offset	EA = (An) + (Xn) + d_8
Immediate Data Addressing	
Immediate	DATA = Next Word(s)
Quick Immediate	Inherent Data
Implied Addressing	
Implied Register	EA = SR, USP, SSP, PC, VBR, SFC, DFC

NOTES:
EA = Effective Address
An = Address Register
Dn = Data Register
Xn = Address or Data Register used as Index Register
SR = Status Register
PC = Program Counter
( ) = Contents of
d_8 = 8-Bit Offset (Displacement)
d_{16} = 16-Bit Offset (Displacement)
N = 1 for byte, 2 for word, and 4 for long word. If An is the stack pointer and the operand size is byte, N = 2 to keep the stack pointer on a word boundary.
← = Replaces

The M68000 instruction set is shown in Table 1-2. Some additional instructions are variations or subsets of these and they appear in Table 1-3. Special emphasis has been given to the instruction set's support of structured high-level languages to facilitate ease of programming. Each instruction, with a few exceptions, operates on bytes, words, and long words and most instructions can use any of the 14 addressing modes. Combining instruction types, data types, and addressing modes, over 1000 useful instructions are provided. These instructions include signed and unsigned multiply and divide, "quick" arithmetic operations, BCD arithmetic, and expanded operations (through traps). Additionally, its high-symmetric, proprietary microcoded structure provides a sound, flexible base for the future.

Table 1-2. Instruction Set Summary

Mnemonic	Description
ABCD*	Add Decimal with Extend
ADD*	Add
AND*	Logical And
ASL*	Arithmetic Shift Left
ASR*	Arithmetic Shift Right
B$_{CC}$	Branch Conditionally
BCHG	Bit Test and Change
BCLR	Bit Test and Clear
BRA	Branch Always
BSET	Bit Test and Set
BSR	Branch to Subroutine
BTST	Bit Test
CHK	Check Register Against Bounds
CLR*	Clear Operand
CMP*	Compare
DB$_{CC}$	Decrement and Branch Conditionally
DIVS	Signed Divide
DIVU	Unsigned Divide
EOR*	Exclusive Or
EXG	Exchange Registers
EXT	Sign Extend
JMP	Jump
JSR	Jump to Subroutine
LEA	Load Effective Address
LINK	Link Stack
LSL*	Logical Shift Left
LSR*	Logical Shift Right

Mnemonic	Description
MOVE*	Move Source to Destination
MOVEC	Move Control Register
MULS	Signed Multiply
MULU	Unsigned Multiply
NBCD*	Negate Decimal with Extend
NEG*	Negate
NOP	No Operation
NOT*	One's Complement
OR*	Logical Or
PEA	Push Effective Address
RESET	Reset External Devices
ROL*	Rotate Left without Extend
ROR*	Rotate Right without Extend
ROXL*	Rotate Left with Extend
ROXR*	Rotate Right with Extend
RTD	Return and Deallocate
RTE	Return from Exception
RTR	Return and Restore
RTS	Return from Subroutine
SBCD*	Subtract Decimal with Extend
S$_{CC}$	Set Conditional
STOP	Stop
SUB*	Subtract
SWAP	Swap Data Register Halves
TAS	Test and Set Operand
TRAP	Trap
TRAPV	Trap on Overflow
TST*	Test
UNLK	Unlink

*These instructions available in loop mode on MC68010. See
APPENDIX G MC68010 LOOP MODE OPERATION.

Table 1-3. Variations of Instruction Types

Instruction Type	Variation	Description
ADD	ADD*	Add
	ADDA*	Add Address
	ADDQ	Add Quick
	ADDI	Add Immediate
	ADDX*	Add with Extend
AND	AND*	Logical And
	ANDI	And Immediate
	ANDI to CCR	And Immediate to Condition Codes
	ANDI to SR	And Immediate to Status Register
CMP	CMP*	Compare
	CMPA*	Compare Address
	CMPM*	Compare Memory
	CMPI	Compare Immediate
EOR	EOR*	Exclusive Or
	EORI	Exclusive Or Immediate
	EORI to CCR	Exclusive Or Immediate to Condition Codes
	EORI to SR	Exclusive Or Immediate to Status Register

Instruction Type	Variation	Description
MOVE	MOVE*	Move Source to Destination
	MOVEA*	Move Address
	MOVEC	Move Control Register
	MOVEM	Move Multiple Registers
	MOVEP	Move Peripheral Data
	MOVEQ	Move Quick
	MOVES	Move Alternate Address Space
	MOVE from SR	Move from Status Register
	MOVE to SR	Move to Status Register
	MOVE from CCR	Move from Condition Codes
	MOVE to CCR	Move to Condition Codes
	MOVE USP	Move User Stack Pointer
NEG	NEG*	Negate
	NEGX*	Negate with Extend
OR	OR*	Logical Or
	ORI	Or Immediate
	ORI to CCR	Or Immediate to Condition Codes
	ORI to SR	Or Immediate to Status Register
SUB	SUB*	Subtract
	SUBA*	Subtract Address
	SUBI	Subtract Immediate
	SUBQ	Subtract Quick
	SUBX*	Subtract with Extend

*These instructions available in loop mode on MC68010. See
APPENDIX G MC68010 LOOP MODE OPERATION.

1.3 SOFTWARE DEVELOPMENT

Many innovative features have been incorporated to make programming easier, faster, and more reliable.

1.3.1 CONSISTENT STRUCTURE.

1.3.1 CONSISTENT STRUCTURE. The highly regular structure of the M68000 greatly simplifies the effort required to write programs in assembly language as well as high-level languages. Operations on integer data in registers and memory are independent of the data. Separate special instructions that operate on byte (8 bit), word (16 bit), and long word (32 bit) integers are not necessary. The progammer need only remember one mnemonic for each type of operation and then specify data size, source addressing mode, and destination addressing mode. This has helped keep the total number of instructions small.

The dual operand nature of many of the instructions significantly increases the flexibility and power of the M68000. Consistency is again maintained since all data registers and memory locations may be either a source or destination for most operations on integer data.

The addressing modes have been kept simple without sacrificing efficiency. All fourteen addressing modes operate consistently and are independent of the instruction operation itself. Additionally, all address registers may be used for the direct, register indirect, and indexed addressing modes (immediate, program counter relative, and absolute addressing by definition do not use address registers). For increased flexibility, any address or data register may be used as an index register. Address register consistency is maintained for stacking operations since any of the eight address registers may be utilized as user program stack pointers with the register indirect postincrement/predecrement addressing modes. Address register A7, however, is a special register that, in addition to its normal addressing capability, functions as the system stack pointer for stacking the program counter for subroutine calls as well as stacking the program counter and status register for traps and interrupts (while in the supervisor state).

1.3.2. STRUCTURED MODULAR PROGRAMMING. The art of programming microprocessors has evolved rapidly in the past few years. Numerous advanced techniques have been developed to allow easier, more consistent and reliable generation of software. In general, these techniques require that the programmer be more disciplined in observing a defined programming structure such as modular programming. Modular programming allows a required function or process to be broken down in short modules or subroutines that are concisely defined and easily programmed and tested. Such a technique is greatly simplified by the availability of advanced structured assemblers and block structured high-level languages such as Pascal. Such concepts are virtually useless, however, unless parameters are easily transferred between and within software modules that operate on a reentrant and recursive basis. (To be reentrant a routine must be usable by interrupt and non-interrupt driven programs without the loss of data. A recursive routine is one that may call or use itself.) The M68000 provides the necessary architectural features to allow efficient reentrant modular programming. The LINK and UNLK instructions reduce subroutine call overhead in two complementary instructions by allowing the manipulation of linked lists of data areas on the stack. The MOVEM

(Move Multiple Register) instruction also reduces subroutine call programming overhead. This allows moving, via an effective address, multiple registers that are specified by the programmer. Sixteen software trap vectors are provided with the TRAP instruction and are useful in operating system call routines or user generated macro routines. Other instructions that support modern structured programming techniques are PEA (Push Effective Address), LEA (Load Effective Address), RTR (Return and Restore), RTE (Return from Exception) as well as JSR, BSR, and RTS.

The powerful vectored priority interrupt structure of the microprocessor allows straight-forward generation of reentrant modular input/output routines. Seven maskable levels of priority with 192 vector locations and seven autovector locations provide maximum flexibility for I/O control (a total of 255 vector locations are available for interrupts, hardware traps, and software traps).

1.3.3. IMPROVED SOFTWARE TESTIBILITY.
The M68000 incorporates several features that reduce the chance for errors. Some of these features, such as consistent architecture and the structured modular programming capability, have already been discussed.

Of major importance to the system programmer are features that have been incorporated specifically to detect the occurrence of programming errors or bugs. Several hardware traps, provided to indicate abnormal internal conditions, detect the following error conditions:
- Word Access with an Odd Address
- Illegal Instructions
- Unimplemented Instructions
- Illegal Memory Access (Bus Error)
- Divide by Zero
- Overflow Condition Code (Separate Instruction TRAPV)
- Register Out of Bounds (CHK Instruction)
- Spurious Interrupt

Additionally, the sixteen software TRAP instructions may be utilized by the programmer to provide applications-oriented error detection or correction routines.

An additional error detection tool is the CHK (Check Register Against Bounds) instruction used for array bound checking by verifying that a data register contains a valid subscript. A trap occurs if the register contents are negative or greater than a limit.

Finally, the M68000 includes a facility that allows instruction-by-instruction tracing of a program being debugged. This trace mode results in a trap being made to a tracing routine after each instruction executed. The trace mode is available to the programmer when the microprocessor is in the supervisor state as well as the user state but may only be entered while in the supervisor state. The supervisor/user states provide an additional degree of error protection for the microprocessor by allowing memory protection of selected areas of memory when an external memory management device is used.

1.4 VIRTUAL MEMORY/MACHINE CONCEPTS

The MC68010 introduced the virtual memory/machine concept of the M68000 architecture.

In most systems using the MC68010 as the central processor, only a fraction of the 16 megabyte address space will actually contain physical memory. However, by using virtual memory techniques the system can be made to appear to the user to have 16 megabytes of physical memory available to him/her. These techniques have been used for several years in large mainframe computers and more recently in minicomputers and now, with the MC68010, can be fully supported in microprocessor-based systems.

In a virtual memory system, a user program can be written as though it has a large amount of memory available to it when only a small amount of memory is physically present in the system. In a similar fashion, a system can be designed in such a manner as to allow user programs to access other types of devices that are not physically present in the system such as tape drives, disk drives, printers, or CRTs. With proper software emulation, a physical system can be made to appear to a user program as any other computer system and the program may be given full access to all of the resources of that emulated system. Such an emulated system is called a virtual machine.

1.4.1 VIRTUAL MEMORY. The basic mechanism for supporting virtual memory in computers is to provide only a limited amount of high-speed physical memory that can be accessed directly by the processor while maintaining an image of a much larger "virtual" memory on secondary storage devices such as large capacity disk drives. When the processor attempts to access a location in the virtual memory map that is not currently residing in physical memory (referred to as a page fault), the access to that location is temporarily suspended while the necessary data is fetched from the secondary storage and placed in physical memory; the suspended access is then completed. The MC68010 provides hardware support for virtual memory with the capability of suspending an instruction's execution when a bus error is signaled and then completing the instruction after the physical memory has been updated as necessary.

The MC68010 uses instruction continuation rather than instruction restart to support virtual memory. With instruction restart, the processor must remember the exact state of the system before each instruction is started in order to restore that state if a page fault occurs during its execution. Then, after the page fault has been repaired, the entire instruction that caused the fault is reexecuted. With instruction continuation, when a page fault occurs the processor stores its internal state and then after the page fault is repaired, restores that internal state and continues execution of the instruction. In order for the MC68010 to utilize instruction continuation, it stores its internal state on the supervisor stack when a bus cycle is terminated with a bus error signal. It then loads the program counter from vector table entry number two (offset $008) and resumes program execution at that new address. When the bus error exception handler routine has completed execution, an RTE instruction is executed which reloads the MC68010 with the internal state stored on the stack, re-runs the faulted bus cycle, and continues the suspended instruction. Instruction continuation has the additional advantage of allowing hardware support for virtual I/O devices. Since virtual registers may be simulated in the memory map, an access to such a register will cause a fault and the function of the register can be emulated by software.

1.4.2 VIRTUAL MACHINE. One typical use for a virtual machine system is in the development of software such as an operating system for another machine with hardware also under development and not available for programming use. In such a system, the governing operating system emulates the hardware of the new system and allows the operating system to be executed and debugged as though it were running on the new hardware. Since the new operating system is controlled by the governing operating system, the new one must execute at a lower privilege level than the governing operating system, so that any attempts by the new operating system to use virtual resources that are not physically present, and should be emulated, will be trapped by the governing operating system and handled in software. In the MC68010, a virtual machine may be fully supported by running the new operating system in the user mode and the governing operating system in the supervisor mode so that any attempts to access supervisor resources or execute privileged instructions by the new operating system will cause a trap to the governing operating system.

In order to fully support a virtual machine, the MC68010 must protect the supervisor resources from access by user programs. The one supervisor resource that is not fully protected in the MC68000 is the system byte of the status register. In the MC68000 and MC68008, the MOVE from SR instruction allows user programs to test the S bit (in addition to the T bit and interrupt mask) and thus determine that they are running in the user mode. For full virtual machine support, a new operating system must not be aware of the fact that it is running in the user mode and thus should not be allowed to access the S bit. For this reason, the MOVE from SR instruction has been added to allow user program unhindered access to the condition codes. By making the MOVE from SR instruction privileged, when the new operating system attempts to access the S bit, a trap to the governing operating system will occur, and the SR image passed to the new operating system by the governing operating system will have the S bit set.

1.5 REFERENCE DOCUMENTATION

Electrical and mechanical information for the three microprocessors covered in this reference manual is available in the individual data sheets listed below.

Title	Ref. No.
MC68000 16-Bit Microprocessor	ADI-814
MC68008 16-Bit Microprocessor with 8-Bit Data Bus	ADI-939
MC68010 16-Bit Virtual Memory Microprocessor	ADI-942

Consult your nearest Motorola Sales Office or franchised distributor for a copy of the desired data sheet. Single copies are also available from the Motorola Semiconductor Products Literature Distribution Center, P.O. Box 20924, Phoenix, Arizona 85306. Their telephone number is (602)994-6561.

SECTION 2
DATA ORGANIZATION AND
ADDRESSING CAPABILITIES

2.1 INTRODUCTION

This section describes the data organization and addressing capabilities of the M68000 architecture.

2.2 OPERAND SIZE

Operand sizes are defined as follows: a byte equals 8 bits, a word equals 16 bits, and a long word equals 32 bits. The operand size for each instruction is either explicitly encoded in the instruction or implicitly defined by the instruction operation. All explicit instructions support byte, word, or long word operands. Implicit instructions support some subset of all three sizes.

2.3 DATA ORGANIZATION IN REGISTERS

The eight data registers support data operands of 1, 8, 16, or 32 bits. The seven address registers together with the active stack pointer support address operands of 32 bits.

2.3.1 DATA REGISTERS. Each data register is 32 bits wide. Byte operands occupy the low order 8 bits, word operands the low order 16 bits, and long word operands the entire 32 bits. The least significant bit is addressed as bit zero; the most significant bit is addressed as bit 31.

When a data register is used as either a source or destination operand, only the appropriate low order portion is changed; the remaining high-order portion is neither used nor changed.

2.3.2. ADDRESS REGISTERS. Each address register and the stack pointer is 32 bits wide and holds a full 32 bit address. Address registers do not support byte sized operands. Therefore, when an address register is used as a source operand, either the low order word or the entire long word operand is used depending upon the operation size. When an address register is used as the destination operand, the entire register is affected regardless of the operation size. If the operation size is word, any other operands are sign extended to 32 bits before the operation is performed.

2.4 DATA ORGANIZATION IN MEMORY

Bytes are individually addressable with the high order byte having an even address the same as the word as shown in Figure 2-1. The low order byte has an odd address that is one count higher than the word address. Instructions and multibyte data are accessed only on word (even byte) boundaries. If a long word datum is located at address n (n even), then the second word of that datum is located at address n + 2.

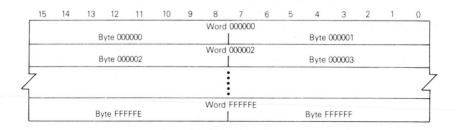

Figure 2-1. Word Organization In Memory

The data types supported by the M68000 are: bit data, integer data of 8, 16, and 32 bits, 32-bit addresses, and binary coded decimal data. Each of these data types is put in memory as shown in Figure 2-2. The numbers indicate the order in which the data would be accessed from the processor. For convenience, the organization of data in memory for the MC68008 is shown in Figure 2-3. The appearance to the programmer, however, is identical to the MC68000 and MC68010.

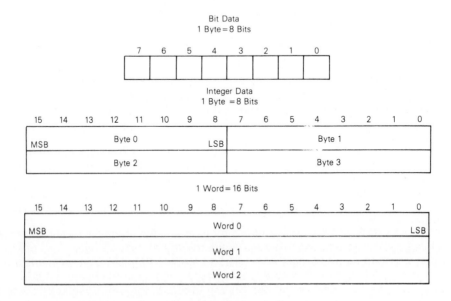

Figure 2-2. Data Organization In Memory (Sheet 1 of 2)

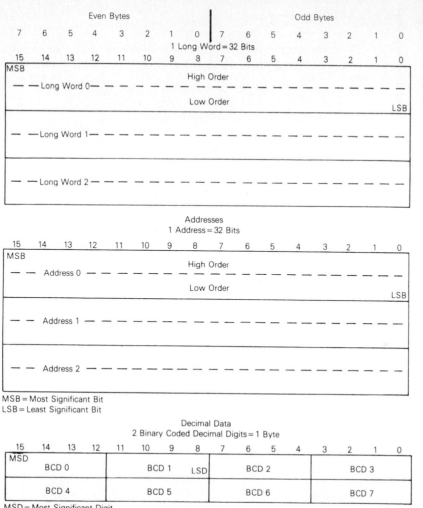

MSB = Most Significant Bit
LSB = Least Significant Bit

MSD = Most Significant Digit
LSD = Least Significant Digit

Figure 2-2. Data Organization In Memory (Sheet 2 of 2)

2.5 ADDRESSING

Instructions for the M68000 contain two kinds of information: the type of function to be performed and the location of the operand(s) on which to perform that function. The methods used to locate (address) the operand(s) are explained in the following paragraphs.

Instructions specify an operand location in one of three ways:
- Register Specification — the number of the register is given in the register field of the instruction.
- Effective Address — use of the different effective address modes.
- Implicit Reference — the definition of certain instructions implies the use of specific registers.

13

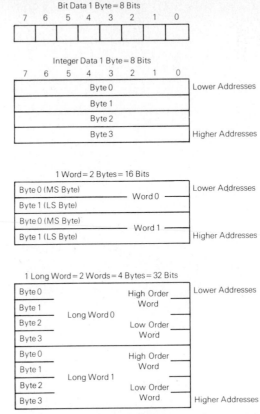

Figure 2-3. Memory Data Organization of the MC68008

2.6 INSTRUCTION FORMAT

Instructions are from one to five words in length as shown in Figure 2-4. The length of the instruction and the operation to be performed is specified by the first word of the instruction which is called the operation word. The remaining words further specify the operands. These words are either immediate operands or extensions to the effective address mode specified in the operation word.

14

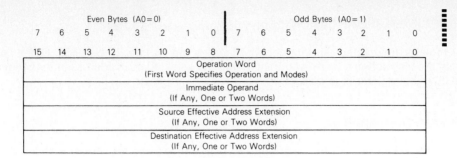

Figure 2-4. Instruction Format

2.7 PROGRAM/DATA REFERENCES

The M68000 separates memory references into two classes: program references and data references. Program references, as the name implies, are references to that section of memory that contains the program being executed. Data references refer to that section of memory that contains data. Generally, operand reads are from the data space. All operand writes are to the data space.

2.8 REGISTER NOTATION

Appendix B contains a definition of the register transfer language (RTL) used in describing instruction operations. The RTL description of registers identifies the registers as follows:

An — Address Register (n specifies the register number)
Dn — Data Register (n specifies the register number)
Rn — Any Register, Address or Data (n specifies the register number)
PC — Program Counter
SR — Status Register
CCR — Condition Code Half of the Status Register
SP — The Active Stack Pointer (either user or supervisor)
USP — User Stack Pointer
SSP — Supervisor Stack Pointer
d — Displacement Value
N — Operand Size in Bytes (1, 2, 4)

2.9 ADDRESS REGISTER INDIRECT NOTATION

When an address register is used to point to a memory location, the addressing mode is called address register indirect. The term indirect is used because the operation of the instruction is not directed to the address itself, but to the memory location pointed to by the adddress register. The RTL symbol for the indirect mode is an address register designation in parenthesis.

2.10 REGISTER SPECIFICATION

The register field within an instruction specifies the register to be used. Other fields within the instruction specify whether the register selected is an address or data register and how the register is to be used.

2.11 EFFECTIVE ADDRESS

Most instructions specify the location of an operand by using the effective address field in the operation word. For example, Figure 2-5 shows the general format of the single effective address instruction operation word. The effective address is composed of two 3-bit fields: the mode field and the register field. The value in the mode field selects the different address modes. The register field contains the number of a register.

The effective address field may require additional information to fully specify the operand. This additional information, called the effective address extension, is contained in a following word or words and is considered part of the instruction as shown in Figure 2-4. The effective address modes are grouped into three categories: register direct, memory addressing, and special.

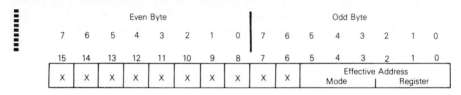

Figure 2-5. Single-Effective-Address-Instruction Operation — General Format

2.11.1 REGISTER DIRECT MODES. These effective addressing modes specify that the operand is in one of the 16 multifunction registers.

2.11.1.1. Data Register Direct. The operand is in the data register specified by the effective address register field.

Generation:	EA = Dn
Assembler Syntax:	Dn
Mode:	000
Register:	n

Data Register Dn

> Operand

2.11.1.2. Address Register Direct. The operand is in the address register specified by the effective address register field.

Generation:	EA = An
Assembler Syntax:	An
Mode:	001
Register:	n

Address Register An

> Operand

16

2.11.2 MEMORY ADDRESS MODES. These effective addressing modes specify that the operand is in memory and provide the specific address of the operand.

2.11.2.1 Address Register Indirect. The address of the operand is in the address register specified by the register field. The reference is classified as a data reference with the exception of the jump and jump to subroutine instructions.

Generation: EA = (An)
Assembler Syntax: (An)
Mode   010
Register   n

Address Register An

Memory Address

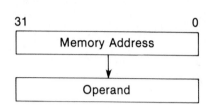

2.11.2.2 Address Register Indirect With Postincrement. The address of the operand is in the address register specified by the register field. After the operand address is used, it is incremented by one, two, or four depending upon whether the size of the operand is byte, word, or long word. If the address register is the stack pointer and the operand size is byte, the address is incremented by two rather than one to keep the stack pointer on a word boundary. The reference is classified as a data reference.

Generation: EA = (An)
                     An = An + N   Mode: 011
Assembler Syntax: (An) +   Register: n

Address Register An

Operand Length (1, 2, or 4)

Memory Address

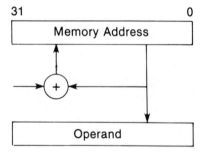

2.11.2.3 Address Register Indirect With Predecrement. The address of the operand is in the address register specified by the register field. Before the operand address is used, it is decremented by one, two, or four depending upon whether the operand size is byte, word, or long word. If the address register is the stack pointer and the operand size is byte, the address is decremented by two rather than one to keep the stack pointer on a word boundary. The reference is classified as a data reference.

Generation: An = An – N
                     EA = (An)   Mode: 100
Assembler Syntax: – (An)   Register: n

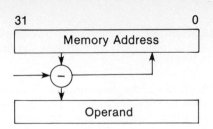

Address Register An

Operand Length (1, 2, or 4)

Memory Address

2.11.2.4 Address Register Indirect With Displacement. This address mode requires one word of extension. The address of the operand is the sum of the address in the address register and the sign-extended 16-bit displacement integer in the extension word. The reference is classified as a data reference with the exception of the jump and jump to subroutine instructions.

Generation: $EA = (An) + d$
Assembler Syntax: $d_{16}(An)$
Mode: 101
Register: n

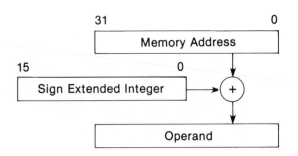

Address Register An

Displacement

Memory Address

2.11.2.5 Address Register Indirect With Index. This address mode requires one word of extension formatted as shown below.

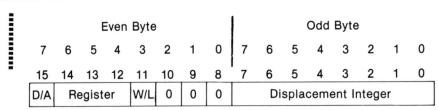

Bit 15 — Index Register Indicator
   0 — data register
   1 — address register
Bits 14 through 12 — Index Register Number
Bit 11 — Index Size
   0 — sign-extended, low order integer in index register
   1 — long value in index register

The address of the operand is the sum of the address in the address register, the sign-extended displacement integer in the low order eight bits of the extension word, and the contents of the index register. The reference is classified as a data reference with the exception of the jump and jump to subroutine instructions. The size of the index register does not affect the execution time of the instructions.

Generation: $EA = (An) + (Ri) + d$ Mode: 110
Assembler Syntax: $d_8(An, Rn.W)$ Register: n
                       $d_8(An, Rn.L)$

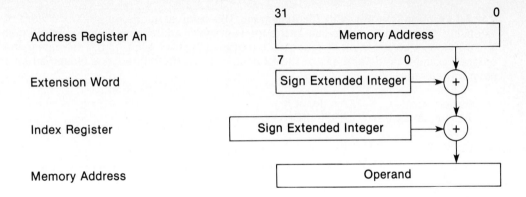

Address Register An

Extension Word

Index Register

Memory Address

2.11.3 SPECIAL ADDRESS MODES. The special address modes use the effective address register field to specify the special addressing mode instead of a register number.

2.11.3.1 Absolute Short Address. This address mode requires one word of extension. The address of the operand is in the extension word. The 16-bit address is sign extended before it is used. The reference is classified as a data reference with the excepion of the jump and jump to subroutine instructions.

Generation:	EA given
Assembler Syntax:	xxx.W
Mode:	111
Register:	000

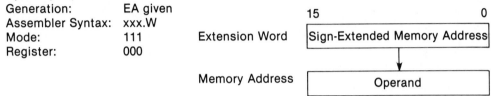

Extension Word

Memory Address

2.11.3.2 Absolute Long Address. The address mode requires two words of extension. The address of the operand is developed by the concatenation of the extension words. The high-order part of the address is the first extension word; the low order part of the address is the second extension word. The reference is classified as a data reference with the exception of the jump and jump to subroutine instructions.

Generation:	EA given
Assembler Syntax:	xxx.L
Mode:	111
Register:	001

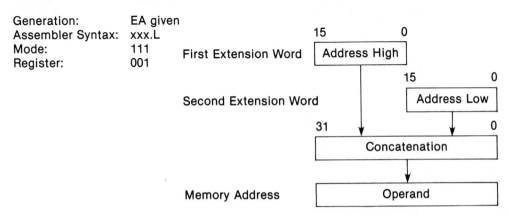

First Extension Word

Second Extension Word

Memory Address

2.11.3.3 Program Counter With Displacement. This address mode requires one word of extension. The address of the operand is the sum of the address in the program counter and the sign-extended 16-bit displacement integer in the extension word. The value in the program counter is the address of the extension word. The reference is classified as a program reference.

Generation: EA = (PC) + d
Assembler Syntax: LABEL (PC)
Mode: 111
Register: 010

Program Counter

Extension Word

Memory Address

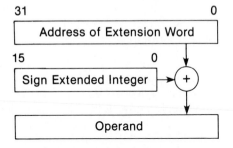

2.11.3.4 Program Counter With Index. This address mode requires one word of extension formatted as shown below.

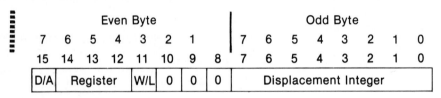

Bit 15 — Index Register Indicator
  0 — data register
  1 — address register
Bits 14 through 12 — Index Register Number
Bit 11 — Index Size
  0 — sign-extended, low order word integer in index register
  1 — long value in index register

The address is the sum of the address in the program counter, the sign-extended displacement integer in the lower eight bits of the extension word, and the contents of the index register. The value in the program counter is the address of the extension word. This reference is classified as a program reference. The size of the index register does not affect the execution time of the instruction.

Generation: EA = (PC) + (Ri) + d
Assembler Syntax: LABEL (PC, Rn.W)
                  LABEL (PC, Rn.L)
Mode: 111
Register: 011

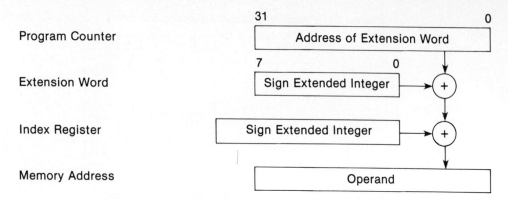

Program Counter

Extension Word

Index Register

Memory Address

2.11.3.5 Immediate Data. This address mode requires either one or two words of extension depending on the size of the operation.

Byte Operation — operand is low order byte of extension word

Word Operation — operand is extension word

Long Word Operation — operand is in the two extension words, high order 16-bits are in the first extension word, low order 16 bits are in the second extension word.

Generation:	Operand given
Assembler Syntax:	#xxxx
Mode:	111
Register:	100

The extension word formats are shown below:

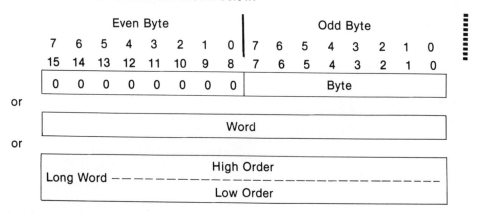

2.11.4 EFFECTIVE ADDRESS ENCODING SUMMARY. Table 2-1 is a summary of the effective addressing modes discussed in the previous paragraphs.

2.12 IMPLICIT REFERENCE

Some instructions make implicit reference to the program counter (PC), the system stack pointer (SP), the supervisor stack pointer (SSP), the user stack pointer (USP), or the status register (SR). Table 2-2 provides a list of these instructions and the registers implied.

Table 2-1. Effective Address Encoding Summary

Addressing Mode	Mode	Register
Data Register Direct	000	register number
Address Register Direct	001	register number
Address Register Indirect	010	register number
Address Register Indirect with Postincrement	011	register number
Address Register Indirect with Predecrement	100	register number
Address Register Indirect with Displacement	101	register number
Address Register Indirect with Index	110	register number
Absolute Short	111	000
Absolute Long	111	001
Program Counter with Displacement	111	010
Program Counter with Index	111	011
Immediate	111	100

Table 2-2. Implicit Instruction Reference Summary

Instruction	Implied Register(s)
Branch Conditional (Bcc), Branch Always (BRA)	PC
Branch to Subroutine (BSR)	PC, SP
Check Register Against Bounds (CHK)	SSP, SR
Test Condition, Decrement and Branch (DBcc)	PC
Signed Divide (DIVS)	SSP, SR
Unsigned Divide (DIVU)	SSP, SR
Jump (JMP)	PC
Jump to Subroutine (JSR)	PC, SP
Link and Allocate (JSR)	PC, SP
Move Condition Codes (MOVE CCR)	SR
Move Control Register (MOVEC)	VBR, SFC, DFC
Move Alternate Address Space (MOVES)	SFC, DFC
Move Status Register (MOVE SR)	SR
Move User Stack Pointer (MOVE USP)	USP
Push Effective Address (PEA)	SP
Return and Deallocate (RTD)	PC, SP
Return from Exception (RTE)	PC, SP, SR
Return and Restore Condition Codes (RTR)	PC, SP, SR
Return from Subroutine (RTS)	PC, SP
Trap (TRAP)	SSP, SR
Trap on Overflow (TRAPV)	SSP, SR
Unlink (UNLK)	SP
Logical Immediate to CCR	SR
Logical Immediate to SR	SR

2.13 STACK AND QUEUES

In addition to supporting the array data structure with the index addressing mode, the M68000 also supports stack and queue data structures with the address register indirect postincrement and predecrement addressing modes. A stack is a last-in-first-out (LIFO) list, a queue is a first-in-first-out (FIFO) list. When data is added to a stack or queue, it is "pushed" onto the structure; when it is removed, it is "pulled" from the structure.

The system stack is used implicitly by many instructions; user stacks and queues may be created and maintained through the addressing modes.

2.13.1 SYSTEM STACK. Address register seven (A7) is the system stack pointer (SP). The system stack pointer is either the supervisor stack pointer (SSP) or the user stack pointer (USP), depending on the state of the S bit in the status register. If the S bit indicates supervisor state, the SSP is the active system stack pointer and the USP cannot be referenced as an address register. If the S bit indicates user state, the USP is the active system stack pointer and the SSP cannot be referenced. Each system stack fills from high memory to low memory. The address mode −(SP) creates a new item on the active system stack and the address mode (SP)+ deletes an item from the active system stack.

The program counter is saved on the active system stack on subroutine calls and restored from the active system stack on returns. On the other hand, both the program counter and the status register are saved on the supervisor stack during the processing of traps and interrupts. Thus, the correct execution of the supervisor state code is not dependent on the behavior of user code and user programs may use the user stack pointer arbitrarily.

In order to keep data on the system stack aligned properly, data entry on the stack is restricted so that data is always put in the stack on a word boundary. Thus, byte data is pushed on or pulled from the system stack in the high half of the word; the lower half is unchanged.

2.13.2 USER STACKS. User stacks can be implemented and manipulated by employing the address register indirect with postincrement and predecrement addressing modes. Using an address register (one of A0 through A6), the user may implement stacks which are filled either from high memory to low memory, or vice versa. The important things to remember are:

- using predecrement, the register is decremented before its contents are used as the pointer into the stack;
- using postincrement, the register is incremented after its contents are used as the pointer into the stack;
- byte data must be put on the stack in pairs when mixed with word or long data so that the stack will not get misaligned when the data is retrieved. Word and long accesses must be on word boundary (even) addresses.

Stack growth from high to low memory is implemented with
 − (An) to push data on the stack,
 (An)+ to pull data from the stack.

After either a push or a pull operation, register An points to the last (top) item on the stack. This is illustrated as:

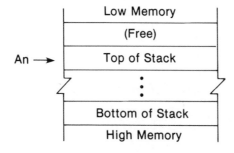

Stack growth from low to high memory is implemented with
  (An)+ to push data on the stack,
  −(An) to pull data from the stack.

After either a push or pull operation, register An points to the next available space on the stack. This is illustrated as:

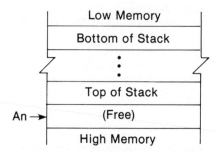

2.13.3 QUEUES. User queues can be implemented and manipulated with the address register indirect with postincrement or predecrement addressing modes. Using a pair of address registers (two of A0 through A6), the user may implement queues which are filled either from high memory to low memory, or vice versa. Because queues are pushed from one end and pulled from the other, two registers are used: the put and get pointers.

Queue growth from low to high memory is implelmented with
  (An)+ to put data into the queue,
  (An)+ to get data from the queue.

After a put operation, the put address register points to the next available space in the queue and the unchanged get address register points to the next item to remove from the queue. After a get operation, the get address register points to the next item to remove from the queue and the unchanged put address register points to the next available space in the queue. This is illustrated as:

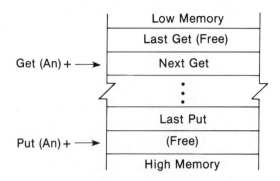

If the queue is to be implemented as a circular buffer, the address register should be checked and, if necessary, adjusted before the put or get operation is performed. The address register is adjusted by subtracting the buffer length (in bytes).

Queue growth from high to low memory is implemented with
   – (An) – to put data into the queue,
   – (An) – to get data from the queue.

After a put operation, the put address register points to the last item put in the queue and the unchanged get address register points to the last item removed from the queue. After a get operation, the get address register points to the last item removed from the queue and the unchanged put address register points to the last item put in the queue. This is illustrated as:

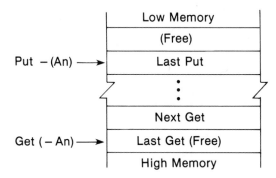

If the queue is to be implemented as a circular buffer, the get or put operation should be performed first, and then the address register should be checked and, if necessary, adjusted. The address register is adjusted by adding the buffer length (in bytes).

SECTION 3
INSTRUCTION SET SUMMARY

3.1 INTRODUCTION

This section contains an overview of the form and structure of the M68000 architecture instruction set. The instructions form a set of tools that include all the machine functions to perform the following operations:

- Data Movement
- Integer Arithmetic
- Logical
- Shift and Rotate
- Bit Manipulation
- Binary Coded Decimal
- Program Control
- System Control

The complete range of instruction capabilities combined with the flexible addressing modes described in Section 2 provide a very flexible base for program development. Detailed information about each instruction is given in Appendix B. Instructions available only on the MC68010 or which behave differently on the MC68010 are highlighted.

3.2 DATA MOVEMENT OPERATIONS

The basic method of data acquisition (transfer and storage) is provided by the move (MOVE) instruction. The move instruction and the effective addressing modes allow both address and data manipulation. Data move instructions allow byte, word, and long word operands to be transferred from memory to memory, memory to register, register to memory, and register to register. Address move instructions allow word and long word operand transfers and ensure that only legal address manipulations are executed. In addition to the general move instruction, there are several special data movement instructions: move multiple registers (MOVEM), move peripheral data (MOVEP), exchange registers (EXG), load effective address (LEA), push effective address (PEA), link stack (LINK), unlink stack (UNLK), and move quick (MOVEQ). Table 3-1 is a summary of the data movement operations.

3.3. INTEGER ARITHMETIC OPERATIONS

The arithmetic operations include the four basic operations of add (ADD), subtract (SUB), multiply (MUL), and divide (DIV) as well as arithmetic compare (CMP), clear (CLR), and negate (NEG). The add and subtract instructions are available for both address and data operations, with data operations accepting all operand sizes. Address operations are limited to legal address size operands (16 or 32 bits). Data, address, and memory compare operations are also available. The clear and negate instructions may be used on all sizes of data operands.

Table 3-1. Data Movement Operations

Instruction	Operand Size	Operation
EXG	32	Rx ←→ Ry
LEA	32	EA → An
LINK	—	(An) → − (SP) (SP) → An (SP) + displacement → SP
MOVE	8, 16, 32	(EA)s → EAd
MOVEC	32	(Rn) → Cr (Cr) → Rn
MOVEM	16, 32	(EA) → An, Dn (An, Dn) → EA
MOVES	8, 16, 32	(EA) → Rn (Rn) → EA

Instruction	Operand Size	Operation
MOVEP	16, 32	d(An) → Dn Dn → d(An)
MOVEQ	8	#xxx → Dn
PEA	32	EA → − (SP)
SWAP	32	Dn[31:16] ←→ Dn[15:0]
UNLK	—	(An) → Sp (SP) + → An

NOTES:
s = source   − ( ) = indirect with predecrement
d = destination   ( ) + = indirect with postdecrement
[ ] = bit numbers   # = immediate data
Cr = Control Register

The multiply and divide operations are available for signed and unsigned operands using word multipy to produce a long product and a long word dividend with word divisor to produce a word quotient with a word remainder.

Multiprecision and mixed size arithmetic can be accomplished using a set of extended instructions. These instructions are: add extended (ADDX), subtract extended (SUBX), sign extend (EXT), and negate binary with extend (NEGX).

A test operand (TST) instruction that will set the condition codes as a result of a compare of the operand with zero is also available. Test and set (TAS) is a synchronization instruction useful in multiprocessor systems. Table 3-2 is a summary of the integer arithmetic operations.

3.4 LOGICAL OPERATIONS

Logical operation instructions AND, OR, EOR, and NOT are available for all sizes of integer data operands. A similar set of immediate instructions (ANDI, ORI, and EORI) provide these logical operations with all sizes of immediate data. Table 3-3 is a summary of the logical operations.

3.5 SHIFT AND ROTATE OPERATIONS

Shift operations in both directions are provided by the arithmetic instructions ASR and ASL and logical shift instructions LSR and LSL. The rotate instructions (with and without extend) available are ROXR, ROXL, ROR, and ROL. All shift and rotate operations can be performed in either registers or memory. Register shifts and rotates support all operand sizes and allow a shift count specified in the instruction of one or eight bits, or 0 to 63 bits specified in a data register.

Memory shifts and rotates are for word operands only and allow single-bit shifts or rotates.

Table 3-4 is a summary of the shift and rotate operations.

Table 3-2. Integer Arithmetic Operations

Instruction	Operand Size	Operation
ADD	8, 16, 32 16, 32	$Dn + (EA) \rightarrow Dn$ $(EA) + Dn \rightarrow (EA)$ $(EA) + \#xxx \rightarrow (EA)$ $An + (EA) \rightarrow An$
ADDX	8, 16, 32 16, 32	$Dx + Dy + X \rightarrow Dx$ $-(Ax) + -(Ay) + X \rightarrow (Ax)$
CLR	8, 16, 32	$0 \rightarrow EA$
CMP	8, 16, 32 16, 32	$Dn - (EA)$ $(EA) - \#xxx$ $(Ax) + -(Ay) +$ $An - (EA)$
DIVS	$32 \div 16$	$Dn \div (EA) \rightarrow Dn$
DIVU	$32 \div 16$	$Dn \div (EA) \rightarrow Dn$
EXT	$8 \rightarrow 16$ $16 \rightarrow 32$	$(Dn)_8 \rightarrow Dn_{16}$ $(Dn)_{16} \rightarrow Dn_{32}$
MULS	$16 \times 16 \rightarrow 32$	$Dn \times (EA) \rightarrow Dn$
MULU	$16 \times 16 \rightarrow 32$	$Dn \times (EA) \rightarrow Dn$
NEG	8, 16, 32	$0 - (EA) \rightarrow (EA)$
NEGX	8, 16, 32	$0 - (EA) - X \rightarrow (EA)$
SUB	8, 16, 32 16, 32	$Dn - (EA) \rightarrow Dn$ $(EA) - Dn \rightarrow (EA)$ $(EA) - \#xxx \rightarrow (EA)$ $An - (EA) \rightarrow An$
SUBX	8, 16, 32	$Dx - Dy - X \rightarrow Dx$ $-(Ax) - -(Ay) - X \rightarrow (Ax)$
TAS	8	$[EA] - 0, 1 \rightarrow EA[7]$
TST	8, 16, 32	$(EA) - 0$

NOTES:
  [ ] = bit number
  − ( ) = indirect with predecrement
  ( ) + = indirect with postdecrement
  # = immediate data

Table 3-3. Logical Operations

Instruction	Operand Size	Operation
AND	8, 16, 32	$Dn \wedge (EA) \rightarrow Dn$ $(EA) \wedge Dn \rightarrow (EA)$ $(EA) \wedge \#xxx \rightarrow (EA)$
OR	8, 16, 32	$Dn \vee (EA) \rightarrow Dn$ $\cdot (EA) \vee Dn \rightarrow (EA)$ $(EA) \vee \#xxx \rightarrow (EA)$
EOR	8, 16, 32	$(EA) \oplus Dy \rightarrow (EA)$ $(EA) \oplus \#xxx \rightarrow (EA)$
NOT	8, 16, 32	$\sim (EA) \rightarrow (EA)$

NOTES:
  $\sim$ = invert V = logical OR
  # = immediate data $\oplus$ = logical exclusive OR
  Λ = logical AND

Table 3-4. Shift and Rotate Operations

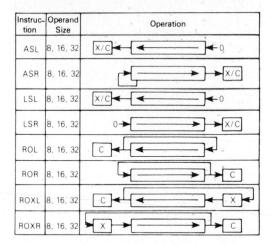

3.6 BIT MANIPULATION OPERATIONS

Bit manipulation operations are accomplished using the following instructions: bit test (BTST), bit test and set (BSET), bit test and clear (BCLR), and bit test and change (BCHG). Table 3-5 is a summary of the bit manipulation operations.

Table 3-5. Bit Manipulation Operations

Instruction	Operand Size	Operation
BTST	8, 32	~ bit of (EA) → Z
BSET	8, 32	~ bit of (EA) → Z 1 → bit of EA
BCLR	8, 32	~ bit of (EA) → Z 0 → bit of EA
BCHG	8, 32	~ bit of (EA) → Z ~ bit of (EA) → bit of EA

NOTE: ~ = invert

3.7 BINARY CODED DECIMAL OPERATIONS

Multiprecision arithmetic operations on binary coded decimal numbers are accomplished using the following instructions: add decimal with extend (ABCD), subtract decimal with extend (SBCD), and negate decimal with extend (NBCD). Table 3-6 is a summary of the binary coded decimal operations.

Table 3-6. Binary Coded Decimal Operations

Instruction	Operand Size	Operation
ABCD	8	$Dx_{10} + Dy_{10} + X \rightarrow Dx$ $-(Ax)_{10} + -(Ay)_{10} + X \rightarrow (Ax)$
SBCD	8	$Dx_{10} - Dy_{10} - X \rightarrow Dx$ $-(Ax)_{10} - -(Ay)_{10} - X \rightarrow (Ax)$
NBCD	8	$0 - (EA)_{10} - X \rightarrow (EA)$

NOTE: $-( ) =$ indirect with predecrement

3.8 PROGRAM CONTROL OPERATIONS

Program control operations are accomplished using a series of conditional and unconditional branch instructions and return instructions. These instructions are summarized in Table 3-7.

The conditional instructions provide setting and branching for the following conditions:

CC — Carry Clear
CS — Carry Set
EQ — Equal
F — Never True
GE — Greater or Equal
GT — Greater Than
HI — High
LE — Less or Equal

LS — Low or Same
LT — Less Than
MI — Minus
NE — Not Equal
PL — Plus
T — Always True
VC — Overflow Clear
VS — Overflow Set

Table 3-7. Program Control Operations

Instruction	Operation
Conditional	
B_{CC}	Branch Conditionally (14 Conditions) 8- and 16-Bit Displacement
DB_{CC}	Test Condition, Decrement, and Branch 16-Bit Displacement
S_{CC}	Set Byte Conditionally (16 Conditions)
Unconditional	
BRA	Branch Always 8- and 16-Bit Displacement
BSR	Branch to Subroutine 8- and 16-Bit Displacement
JMP	Jump
JSR	Jump to Subroutine
Returns	
RTD	Return from Subroutine and and Deallocate Stack
RTR	Return and Restore Condition Codes
RTS	Return from Subroutine

3.9 SYSTEM CONTROL OPERATIONS

System control operations are accomplished by using privileged instructions, trap generating instructions, and instructions that use or modify the status register. These instructions are summarized in Table 3-8. In the MC68010, the MOVE from SR instruction has been made privileged and the MOVE from CCR instruction has been added. See **SECTION 4 EXCEPTION PROCESSING.**

Table. 3-8. System Control Operations

Instruction	Operation
Privileged	
ANDI to SR	Logical AND to Status Register
EORI to SR	Logical EOR to Status Register
MOVE EA to SR	Load New Status Register
MOVE SR to EA	Store Status Register
MOVE USP	Move User Stack Pointer
MOVEC	Move Control Register
MOVES	Move Alternate Address Space
ORI to SR	Logical OR to Status Register
RESET	Reset External Devices
RTE	Return from Exception
STOP	Stop Program Execution
Trap Generating	
CHK	Check Data Register Against Upper Bounds
TRAP	Trap
TRAPV	Trap on Overflow
Condition Code Register	
ANDI to CCR	Logical AND to Condition Codes
EORI to CCR	Logical EOR to Condition Codes
MOVE EA to CCR	Load New Condition Codes
MOVE CCR to EA	Store Condition Codes
ORI to CCR	Logical OR to Condition Codes

SECTION 4
EXCEPTION PROCESSING

4.1 INTRODUCTION

This section describes the actions of the M68000 which are outside the normal processing associated with the execution of instructions. The functions of the bits in the supervisor portion of the status register are covered: the supervisor/user bit, the trace enable bit, and the processor priority mask. Finally, the sequence of memory references and actions taken by the processor on exception conditions is detailed.

The processor is always in one of three processing states: normal, exception, or halted. The normal processing state is that associated with instruction execution; the memory references are to fetch instructions and operands, and to store results. A special case of the normal state is the stopped state which the processor enters when a STOP instruction is executed. In this state, no further memory references are made.

An additional special case of the normal state exists in the MC68010, the loop mode, which may be entered when a DBcc instruction is executed. In loop mode, only operand fetches occur. See **APPENDIX G MC68010 LOOP MODE OPERATION.**

The exception processing state is associated with interrupts, trap instructions, tracing, and other exceptional conditions. The exception may be internally generated by an instruction or by an unusual condition arising during the execution of an instruction. Externally, exception processing can be forced by an interrupt, by a bus error, or by a reset. Exception processing is designed to provide an efficient context switch so that the processor may handle unusual conditions.

The halted processing state is an indication of catastrophic hardware failure. For example, if during the exception processing of a bus error another bus error occurs, the processor assumes that the system is unusable and halts. Only an external reset can restart a halted processor. Note that a processor in the stopped state is not in the halted state, nor vice versa.

4.2 PRIVILEGE STATES

The processor operates in one of two states of privilege: the user state or the supervisor state. The privilege state determines which operations are legal, are used by the external memory management device to control and translate accesses, and are used to choose between the supervisor stack pointer and the user stack pointer in instruction references.

The privilege state is a mechanism for providing security in a computer system. Programs should access only their own code and data areas and ought to be restricted from accessing information which they do not need and must not modify.

The privilege mechanism provides security by allowing most programs to execute in user state. In this state, the accesses are controlled and the effects on other parts of the system are limited. The operating system executes in the supervisor state, has access to all resources, and performs the overhead tasks for the user state programs.

4.2.1 SUPERVISOR STATE. The supervisor state is the higher state of privilege. For instruction execution, the supervisor state is determined by the S bit of the status register; if the S bit is asserted (high), the processor is in the supervisor state. All instructions can be executed in the supervisor state. The bus cycles generated by instructions executed in the supervisor state are classified as supervisor references. While the processor is in the supervisor privilege state, those instructions which use either the system stack pointer implicitly or address register seven explictly access the supervisor stack pointer.

All exception processing is done in the supervisor state, regardless of the state of the S bit when the exception occurs. The bus cycles generated during exception processing are classified as supervisor references. All stacking operations during exception processing use the supervisor stack pointer.

4.2.2 USER STATE. The user state is the lower state of privilege. For instruction execution, the user state is determined by the S bit of the status register; if the S bit is negated (low), the processor is executing instructions in the user state.

Most instructions execute identically in user state and in the supervisor state. However, some instructions which have important system effects are made privileged. User programs are not permitted to execute the STOP instruction or the RESET instruction. To ensure that a user program cannot enter the supervisor state except in a controlled manner, the instructions which modify the whole status register are privileged. To aid in debugging programs which are to be used as operating systems, the move to user stack pointer (MOVE to USP) and move from user stack pointer (MOVE from USP) instructions are also privileged.

To implement virtual machine concepts in the MC68010, the move from status register (MOVE from SR), move to/from control register (MOVEC), and move alternate address space (MOVES) instructions are also privileged.

The bus cycles generated by an instruction executed in user state are classified as user state references. This allows an external memory management device to translate the address and the control access to protected portions of the address space. While the processor is in the user privilege state, those instructions which use either the system stack pointer implicitly or address register seven explicitly access the user stack pointer.

4.2.3 PRIVILEGE STATE CHANGES. Once the processor is in the user state and executing instructions, only exception processing can change the privilege state. During exception processing, the current state of the S bit of the status register is saved and the S bit is asserted, putting the processor in the supervisor state. Therefore, when instruction execution resumes at the address specified to process the exception, the processor is in the supervisor privilege state.

The transition from supervisor to user state can be accomplished by any of four instructions: return from exception (RTE), move to status register (MOVE word to SR), AND immediate to status register (ANDI to SR), and exclusive OR immediate to status register (EORI to SR). The RTE instruction fetches the new status register and program counter from the supervisor stack, loads each into its respective register, and then begins the instruction fetch at the new program counter address in the privilege state determined by the S bit of the new contents of the status register. The MOVE, ANDI, and EORI to status register instructions each fetch all operands in the supervisor state, perform the appropriate update to the status register, and then fetch the next instruction at the next sequential program counter address in the privilege state determined by the new S bit.

4.2.4 REFERENCE CLASSIFICATION. When the processor makes a reference, it classifies the kind of reference being made, using the encoding of the three function code output lines. This allows external translation of addresses, control of access, and differentiation of special processor states, such as interrupt acknowledge. Table 4-1 lists the classification of references.

Table 4-1. Reference Classification

Function Code Output			Reference Class
FC2	FC1	FC0	
0	0	0	(Unassigned)
0	0	1	User Data
0	1	0	User Program
0	1	1	(Unassigned)
1	0	0	(Unassigned)
1	0	1	Supervisor Data
1	1	0	Supervisor Program
1	1	1	Interrupt Acknowledge

4.3 EXCEPTION PROCESSING

Before discussing the details of interrupts, traps, and tracing, a general description of exception processing is in order. The processing of an exception occurs in four steps. with variations for different exception causes. During the first step, a temporary copy of the status register is made and the status register is set for exception processing. In the second step the exception vector is determined and the third step is the saving of the current processor context. In the fourth step a new context is obtained and the processor switches to instruction processing.

4.3.1 EXCEPTION VECTORS. Exception vectors are memory locations from which the processor fetches the address of a routine which will handle that exception. All exception vectors are two words in length (Figure 4-1) except for the reset vector, which is four words. All exception vectors lie in the supervisor data space except for the reset vector which is in the supervisor program space. A vector number is an 8-bit number which, when multiplied by four, gives the offset of an exception vector. Vector numbers are generated internally or externally, depending on the cause of the exception. In the case of interrupts, during the interrupt acknowledge bus cycle, a peripheral provides an 8-bit vector number (Figure 4-2) to the processor on data bus lines D0 through D7.

The processsor forms the vector offset by left-shifting the vector number two bit positions and zero-filling the upper order bits to obtain a 32-bit long word vector offset. In the case of the MC68000 and MC68008, this offset is used as the absolute address to obtain the exception vector itself. This is shown in Figure 4-3.

In the case of the MC68010, the vector offset is added to the 32-bit vector base register (VBR) to obtain the 32-bit absolute address of the exception vector. This is shown in Figure 4-4. Since the VBR is set to zero upon reset, the MC68010 will function identically to the MC68000 and MC68008 until the VBR is changed via the MOVEC instruction.

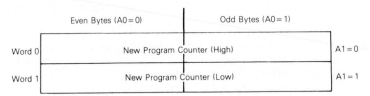

Figure 4-1. Exception Vector Format

Figure 4-2. Peripheral Vector Number Format

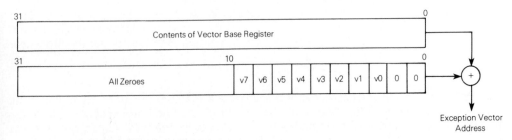

Figure 4-3. Address Translated from 8-Bit Vector Number (MC68000, MC68008)

Figure 4-4. Exception Vector Address Calculation (MC68010)

The actual address output on the address bus is truncated to the number of address bits available on the bus of the particular implementation of the M68000 architecture. In the case of the MC68000 and the MC68010, this is 24 bits. In the case of the MC68008, the address is 20 bits in length. The memory map for exception vectors is given in Table 4-2.

Table 4-2. Exception Vector Assignment

Vector Number(s)	Dec	Address Hex	Space	Assignment
0	0	000	SP	Reset: Initial SSP[2]
1	4	004	SP	Reset: Initial PC[2]
2	8	008	SD	Bus Error
3	12	00C	SD	Address Error
4	16	010	SD	Illegal Instruction
5	20	014	SD	Zero Divide
6	24	018	SD	CHK Instruction
7	28	01C	SD	TRAPV Instruction
8	32	020	SD	Privilege Violation
9	36	024	SD	Trace
10	40	028	SD	Line 1010 Emulator
11	44	02C	SD	Line 1111 Emulator
12[1]	48	030	SD	(Unassigned, Reserved)
13[1]	52	034	SD	(Unassigned, Reserved)
14	56	038	SD	Format Error[5]
15	60	03C	SD	Uninitialized Interrupt Vector
16-23[1]	64	040	SD	(Unassigned, Reserved)
	95	05F		—
24	96	060	SD	Spurious Interrupt[3]
25	100	064	SD	Level 1 Interrupt Autovector
26	104	068	SD	Level 2 Interrupt Autovector
27	108	06C	SD	Level 3 Interrupt Autovector
28	112	070	SD	Level 4 Interrupt Autovector
29	116	074	SD	Level 5 Interrupt Autovector
30	120	078	SD	Level 6 Interrupt Autovector
31	124	07C	SD	Level 7 Interrupt Autovector
32-47	128	080	SD	TRAP Instruction Vectors[4]
	191	0BF		
48-63[1]	192	0C0	SD	(Unassigned, Reserved)
	255	0FF		—
64-255	256	100	SD	User Interrupt Vectors
	1023	3FF		—

NOTES:
1. Vector numbers 12, 13, 16 through 23, and 48 through 63 are reserved for future enhancements by Motorola. No user peripheral devices should be assigned these numbers.
2. Reset vector (0) requires four words, unlike the other vectors which only require two words, and is located in the supervisor program space.
3. The spurious interrupt vector is taken when there is a bus error indication during interrupt processing. Refer to Paragraph 4.4.2.
4. TRAP #n uses vector number 32 + n.
5. MC68010 only. See Return from Exception Section.
   This vector is unassigned, reserved on the MC68000, and MC68008.

As shown in Table 4-2, the memory layout is 512 words long (1024 bytes). It starts at address 0 (decimal) and proceeds through address 1023 (decimal). This provides 255 unique vectors; some of these are reserved for TRAPS and other system functions. Of the 255, there are 192 reserved for user interrupt vectors. However, there is no protection on the first 64 entries, so user interrupt vectors may overlap at the discretion of the systems designer.

4.3.2. KINDS OF EXCEPTONS. Exceptions can be generated by either internal or external causes. The externally generated exceptions are the interrupts and the bus error and reset requests. The interrupts are requests from peripheral devices for processor action while the bus error and reset inputs are used for access control and processor restart. The internally generated exceptions come from instructions, or from address errors, or tracing. The trap (TRAP), trap on overflow (TRAPV), check register against bounds (CHK), and divide (DIV) instructions all can generate exceptions as part of their instruction execution. In addition, illegal instructions, word fetches from odd addresses, and privilege violations cause exceptions. Tracing behaves like a very high priority, internally generated interrupt after each instruction execution.

4.3.3. MULTIPLE EXCEPTIONS. These paragraphs describe the processing which occurs when multiple exceptions arise simultaneously. Exceptions can be grouped according to their occurrence and priority. The group 0 exceptions are reset, bus error, and address error. These exceptions cause the instruction currently being executed to be aborted and the exception processing to commence within two clock cycles. The group 1 exceptions are trace and interrupt, as well as the privilege violations and illegal instructions. These exceptions allow the current instruction to execute to completion, but preempt the execution of the next instruction by forcing exception processing to occur (privilege violations and illegal instructions are detected when they are the next instruction to be executed). The group 2 exceptions occur as part of the normal processing of instructions. The TRAP, TRAPV, CHK, and zero divide exceptions are in this group. For these exceptions, the normal execution of an instruction may lead to exception processing.

Group 0 exceptions have highest priority, while group 2 exceptions have lowest priority. Within group 0, reset has highest priority, followed by bus error and then address error. Within group 1, trace has priority over external interrupts, which in turn takes priority over illegal instruction and privilege violation. Since only one instruction can be executed at a time, there is no priority relation within group 2.

The priority relation between two exceptions determines which is taken, or taken first, if the conditions for both arise simultaneously. Therefore, if a bus error occurs during a TRAP instruction, the bus error takes precedence, and the TRAP instruction processing is aborted. In another example, if an interrupt request occurs during the execution of an instruction while the T bit is asserted, the trace exception has priority, and is processed first. Before instruction execution resumes, however, the interrupt exception is also processed and instruction processing commences finally in the interrupt handler routine. A summary of exception grouping and priority is given in Table 4-3.

Table 4-3. Exception Grouping and Priority

Group	Exception	Processing
0	Reset Address Error Bus Error	Exception processing begins within two clock cycles
1	Trace Interrupt Illegal Privilege	Exception processing begins before the next instruction
2	TRAP, TRAPV, CHK Zero Divide	Exception processing is started by normal instruction execution

4.3.4 EXCEPTION STACK FRAMES. Exception processing saves the most volatile portion of the current processor context on the top of the supervisor stack. This context is organized in a format called the exception stack frame. Although this information varies with the particular processor and type of exception, it always includes the status register and program counter of the processor when the exception occurred.

The amount and type of information saved on the stack is determined by the processor type and type of exception. Exceptions are grouped by type according to priority of the exception. The group 0 exceptions include address error, bus error, and reset. The group 2 and 3 exceptions include interrupts, traps, illegal instructions, and trace.

The MC68000 and MC68008 group 1 and 2 exception stack frame is shown in Figure 4-5. Only the program counter and status register are saved. The program counter points to the next instruction to be executed after exceptions processing.

The MC68010 exception stack frame is shown in Figure 4-6. The number of words actually stacked depends on the exception type. Group 0 exceptions (except reset) stack 29 words and group 1 and 2 exceptions stack four words. In order to support generic exception handlers, the processor also places the vector offset in the exception stack frame. The format code field allows the RTE (return from exception) instruction to identify what information is on the stack so that it may be properly restored. Table 4-4 lists the MC68010 stack format codes. Although some formats are peculiar to a particular M68000 family processor, the format 0000 is always legal and indicates that just the first four words of the frame are present.

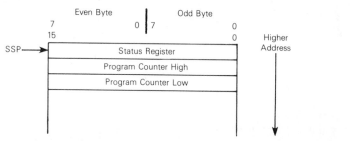

Figure 4-5. MC68000, MC68008 Group 1 and 2 Exception Stack Frame

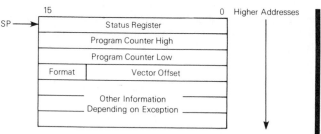

Figure 4-6. MC68010 Stack Frame

Table 4-4. MC68010 Format Codes

Format Code	Stacked Information
0000	MC68010 Short Format (4 Words)
1000	MC68010 Long Format (29 Words)
All Others	Unassigned, Reserved

4.3.5 EXCEPTION PROCESSING SEQUENCE. Exception processing occurs in four iden-
tifiable steps. In the first step, an internal copy is made of the status register. After the
copy is made, the S bit is asserted, putting the processor into the supervisor privilege
state. Also, the T bit is negated, which will allow the exception handler to execute
unhindered by tracing. For the reset and interrupt exceptions, the interrupt priority mask
is also updated.

In the second step, the vector number of the exception is determined. For interrupts, the
vector number is obtained by a processor fetch and classified as an interrupt
acknowledge. For all other exceptions, internal logic provides the vector number. This
vector number is then used to generate the address of the exception vector. Group 1 and
2 exceptions use a short format exception stack frame (format = 0000 on the MC68010).
Additional information defining the current context is stacked for the bus error and address error exceptions.

The third step is to save the current processor status, except for the reset exception. The
current program counter value and the saved copy of the status register are stacked using the supervisor stack pointer. The program counter value stacked usually points to the
next unexecuted instruction, however for bus error and address error, the value stacked
for the program counter is unpredictable and may be incremented from the address of
the instruction which caused the error. Additional information defining the current context is stacked for the bus error and address error exceptions.

The last step is the same for all exceptions. The new program counter value is fetched
from the exception vector. The processor then resumes instruction execution. The instruction at the address given in the exception vector is fetched and normal instruction
decoding and execution is started.

4.4 EXCEPTION PROCESSING DETAILED DISCUSSION

Exceptions have a number of sources and each exception has processing which is
peculiar to it. The following paragraphs detail the source of exceptions, how each arises,
and how each is processed.

4.4.1 RESET. The reset input provides the highest exception level. The processing of the
reset signal is designed for system initiation and recovery from catastrophic failure. Any
processing in progress at the time of the reset is aborted and cannot be recovered. The
processor is forced into the supervisor state and the trace state is forced off. The processor interrupt priority mask is set at level seven. In the MC68010, the vector base
register (VBR) is forced to zero. The vector number is internally generated to reference
the reset exception vector at location 0 in the supervisor program space. Because no

assumptions can be made about the validity of register contents, in particular the supervisor stack pointer, neither the program counter nor the status register is saved. The address contained in the first two words of the reset exception vector is fetched as the initial supervisor stack pointer and the address in the last two words of the reset exception vector is fetched as the initial program counter. Finally, instruction execution is started at the address in the program counter. The power-up/restart code should be pointed to by the initial program counter.

The RESET instruction does not cause loading of the reset vector, but does assert the reset line to reset external devices. This allows the software to reset the system to a known state and then continue processing with the next instruction.

4.4.2. INTERRUPTS. Seven levels of interrupt priorities are provided. In the MC68000 and MC68010, all seven levels are available. The MC68008 supports three interrupt levels: two, five, and seven, level seven being the highest priority. Devices may be chained externally within interrupt priority levels, allowing an unlimited number of peripheral devices to interrupt the processor. Interrupt priority levels are numbered from one to seven, level seven being the highest priority. The status register contains a three-bit mask which indicates the current processor priority and interrupts are inhibited for all priority levels less than or equal to the current processor priority.

An interrupt request is made to the processor by encoding the interrut request level on the interrupt request lines; a zero indicates no interrupt request. Interrupt requests arriving at the processor do not force immediate exception processing, but are made pending. Pending interrupts are detected between instruction executions. If the priority of the pending interrupt is lower than or equal to the current processsor priority, execution continues with the next instruction and the interrupt exception processing is postponed.

If the priority of the pending interrupt is greater than the current processor priority, the exception processing sequence is started. A copy of the status register is saved, the privilege state is set to supervisor state, tracing is suppressed, and the processor priority level is set to the level of the interrupt being acknowledged. The processor fetches the vector number from the interrupting device, classifying the reference as an interrupt acknowledge and displaying the level number of the interrupt being acknowledged on the address bus. If external logic requests automatic vectoring, the processor internally generates a vector number which is determined by the interrupt level number. If external logic indicates a bus error, the interrupt is taken to be spurious, and the generated vector number references the spurious interrupt vector. The processor then proceeds with the usual exception processing, saving the format/offset word (MC68010 only), program counter, and status register on the supervisor stack. The offset value in the format/offset word on the MC68010 is the externally supplied or internally generated vector number multiplied by four. The format will be all zeroes. The saved value of the program counter is the address of the instruction which would have been executed had the interrupt not been present. The content of the interrupt vector whose vector number was previously obtained is fetched and loaded into the program counter, and normal instruction execution commences in the interrupt handling routine.

Priority level seven is a special case. Level seven interrupts cannot be inhibited by the interrupt priority mask, thus providing a "non-maskable interrupt" capability. An interrupt is generated each time the interrupt request level changes from some lower level to level seven. Note that a level seven interrupt may still be caused by the level comparison if the request level is a seven and the processor priority is set to a lower level by an instruction.

4.4.3 UNINITIALIZED INTERRUPT. An interrupting device asserts $\overline{VPA}$, $\overline{BERR}$, or provides and M68000 interrupt vector number and asserts $\overline{DTACK}$ during an interrupt acknowledge cycle by the M68000. If the vector register has not been initialized, the responding M68000 Family peripheral will provide vector number 15, the uninitialized interrupt vector. This provides a uniform way to recover from a programming error.

4.4.4 SPURIOUS INTERRUPT. If during the interrupt acknowledge cycle no device responds by asserting $\overline{DTACK}$ or $\overline{VPA}$, $\overline{BERR}$ should be asserted to terminate the vector acquisition. The processor separates the processing of this error from bus error by forming a short format exception stack and fetching the spurious interrupt vector instead of the bus error vector. The processor then proceeds with the usual exception processing.

4.4.5. INSTRUCTION TRAPS. Traps are exceptions caused by instructions. They arise either from processor recognition of abnormal conditions during instruction, execution, or from use of instructions whose normal behavior is trapping.

Exception processing for traps is straightforward. The status register is copied, the supervisor state is entered, and the trace state is turned off. The vector number is internally generated; for the TRAP instruction, part of the vector number comes from the instruction itself. The program counter and the copy of the status register are saved on the supervisor stack. The saved value of the program counter is the address of the instruction after the instruction which generated the trap. Finally, instruction execution commences at the address contained in the exception vector.

Some instructions are used specifically to generate traps. The TRAP instruction always forces an exception and is useful for implementing system calls for user programs. The TRAPV and CHK instructions force an exception if the user program detects a runtime error, which may be an arithmetic overflow or a subscript out of bounds.

The signed divide (DIVS) and unsigned divide (DIVU) instructions will force an exception if a division operation is attempted with a divisor of zero.

4.4.6 ILLEGAL AND UNIMPLEMENTED INSTRUCTIONS. Illegal instruction is the term used to refer to any of the word bit patterns which are not the bit patterns of the first word of a legal M68000 instruction. During instruction execution, if such an instruction is fetched, an illegal instruction exception occurs. Motorola reserves the right to define instructions whose opcodes may be any of the illegal instructions. Three bit patterns will always force an illegal instruction trap on all M68000 Family compatible microprocessors. They are: $4AFA, $4AFB, and $4AFC. Two of the patterns, $4AFA and $4AFB, are reserved for Motorola system products. The third pattern, $4AFC, is reserved for customer use.

In addition to the previously defined illegal instruction opcodes, the MC68010 defines eight breakpoint illegal instructions with the bit patterns $4848-$484F. These instructions cause the processor to enter illegal instruction exception processing as usual, but a breakpoint bus cycle is executed before the stacking operations are performed in which the function code lines (FC0-2) are high and the address lines are all low. The processor does not accept or send any data during this cycle. Whether the breakpoint cycle is terminated with a $\overline{DTACK}$, $\overline{BERR}$, or $\overline{VPA}$ signal, the processor will continue with the illegal instruction processing. The purpose of this cycle is to provide a software breakpoint that will signal external hardware when it is executed. See MC68010 Advanced Information data sheet.

Word patterns with bits 15 through 12 equaling 1010 or 1111 are distinguished as unimplemented instructions and separate exception vectors are given to these patterns to permit efficient emulation. "Line F" opcodes beginning with bit patterns equaling 1111 are implemented in the MC68020 as co-processor instructions. This facility allows the operating system to detect program errors or to emulate unimplemented instructions in software.

Exception processing for illegal instructions is similar to that for traps. After the instruction is fetched and decoding is attempted, the processor determines that execution of an illegal instruction is being attempted and starts exception processing. The exception stack frame for group 2 is then pushed on the supervisor stack and the illegal instruction vector is fetched.

4.4.7 PRIVILEGE VIOLATIONS. In order to provide system security, various instructions are privileged. An attempt to execute one of the privileged instructions while in the user state will cause an exception. The privileged instructions are:

AND Immediate to SR	MOVE USP
EOR Immediate to SR	OR Immediate to SR
MOVE to SR	RESET
MOVE from SR*	RTE
MOVEC*	STOP
MOVES*	

*MC68010 only

Exception processing for privilege violations is nearly identical to that for illegal instructions. After the instruction is fetched and decoded, and the processor determines that a privilege violation is being attempted, the processor starts exception processing. The status register is copied, the supervisor state is entered, and the trace state is turned off. The vector number is generated to reference the privilege violation vector, and the current program counter and the copy of the status register are saved on the supervisor stack and, if the processor is an MC68010, the format/offset word, is also saved. The saved value of the program counter is the address of the first word of the instruction which caused the privilege violation. Finally, instruction execution commences at the address contained in the privilege violation exception vector.

4.4.8 TRACING. To aid in program development, the MC68000 includes a facility to allow instruction by instruction tracing. In the trace state, after each instruction is executed, an exception is forced, allowing a debugging program to monitor the execution of the program under test.

The trace facility uses the T bit in the supervisor portion of the status register. If the T bit is negated (off), tracing is disabled and instruction execution proceeds from instruction to instruction as normal. If the T bit is asserted (on) at the beginning of the execution of an instruction, a trace exception will be generated after the execution of that instruction is completed. If the instruction is not executed, either because an interrupt is taken or the instruction is illegal or privileged, the trace exception does not occur. The trace exception also does not occur if the instruction is aborted by a reset, bus error, or address error exception. If the instruction is indeed executed and an interrupt is pending on completion, the trace exception is processed before the interrupt exception. If, during the execution of the instruction, an exception is forced by that instruction, the forced exception is processeed before the trace exception.

As an extreme illustration of the above rules, consider the arrival of an interrupt during the exception of a TRAP instruction while tracing is enabled. First the trap exception is processed, then the trace exception, and finally the interrupt exception. Instruction execution resumes in the interrupt handler routine.

The exception processing for trace is quite simple. After the execution of the instruction is completed and before the start of the next instruction, exception processing begins. A copy is made of the status register. The transition to supervisor privilege state is made and, as usual, the T bit of the status register is turned off, disabling further tracing. The vector number is generated to reference the trace exception vector, and the current program counter, the copy of the status register and, on the MC68010, the format/offset word are saved on the supervisor stack. The saved value of the program counter is the address of the next instruction. Instruction execution commences at the address contained in the trace exception vector.

4.4.9 BUS ERROR. Bus error exceptions occur when the external logic requests that a bus error be processed by an exception. The current bus cycle which the processor is making is then aborted. Whether the processor was doing instruction or exception processing, that processing is terminated and the processor immediately begins exception processing.

The bus error facility is identical on the MC68000 and MC68008; however, the stack frame produced on the MC68010 contains more information. This is to allow the instruction continuation facility which can be used to implement virtual memory on the MC68010 processor. Bus error for the MC68000/MC68008 and for the MC68010 are described separately below.

4.4.9.1 Bus Error (MC68000/MC68008). Exception processing for bus error follows the usual sequence of steps. The status register is copied, the supervisor state is entered, and the trace state is turned off. The vector number is generated to refer to the bus error vector. Since the processor was not between instructions when the bus error exception request was made, the context of the processor is more detailed. To save more of this context, additional information is saved on the supervisor stack. The program counter and the copy of the status register are of course saved. The value saved for the program counter is advanced by some amount, two to ten bytes beyond the address of the first word of the instruction which made the reference causing the bus error. If the bus error occurred during the fetch of the next instruction, the saved program counter has a value in the vicinity of the current instruction, even if the current instruction is a branch, a jump, or a return instruction. Besides the usual information, the processor saves its internal copy of the first word of the instruction being processed and the address which was being accessed by the aborted bus cycle. Specific information about the access is also saved: whether it was a read or write, whether the processor was processing an instruction or not, and the classification displayed on the function code ouputs when the bus error occurred. The processor is processing an instruction if it is in the normal state or processing a group 2 exception; the processor is not processing an instruction if it is processing a group 0 or a group 1 exception. Figure 4-7 illustrates how this information is organized on the supervisor stack. If a bus error occurs during the last step of exception processing, while either reading the exception vector or fetching the instruction, the value of the program counter is the address of the exception vector. Although this information is not sufficient in general to effect full recovery from the bus error, it does allow software diagnosis. Finally, the processor commences instruction processing at the address contained in the vector. It is the responsibility of the error handler routine to clean up the stack and determine where to continue execution.

If a bus error occurs during the exception processing for a bus error, address error, or read, the processor is halted, and all processing ceases. This simplifies the detection of a catastrophic system failure, since the processor removes itself from the system rather than destroy all memory contents. Only the RESET pin can restart a halted processor

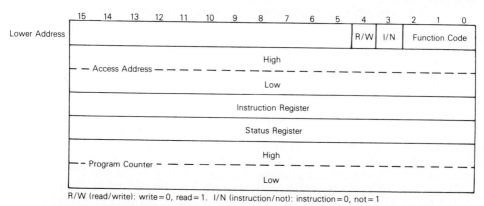

R/W (read/write): write = 0, read = 1. I/N (instruction/not): instruction = 0, not = 1

Figure 4-7. Supervisor Stack Order for Bus or Address Error Exception

4.4.9.2 Bus Error (MC68010). Exception processing for a bus error follows a slightly different sequence than the sequence for group 1 and 2 exceptions. In addition to the four steps executed during exception processing for all other exceptions, 22 words of additional information are placed on the stack. This additional information describes the internal state of the processor at the time of the bus error and is reloaded by the RTE instruction to continue the instruction that caused the error. Figure 4-8 shows the order of the stacked information.

45

SP→	Status Register
	Program Counter (High)
	Program Counter (Low)
1 0 0 0	Vector Offset
	Special Status Word
	Fault Address (High)
	Fault Address (Low)
	UNUSED, RESERVED
	Data Output Buffer
	UNUSED, RESERVED
	Data Input Buffer
	UNUSED, RESERVED
	Instruction Input Buffer
	Internal Information, 16 Words

NOTE: The stack pointer is decremented by 29 words, although only 26 words of information are actually written to memory. The three additional words are reserved for future use by Motorola.

Figure 4-8. Exception Stack Order (Bus and Address Error)

The value of the saved program counter does not necessarily point to the instruction that was executing when the bus error occurred, but may be advanced by up to five words. This is due to the prefetch mechanism on the MC68010 that always fetches a new instruction word as each previously fetched instruction word is used. However, enough information is placed on the stack for the bus error exception handler routine to determine why the bus fault occurred. This additional information includes the address that was being accessed, the function codes for the access, whether it was a read or a write, and what internal register was included in the transfer. The fault address can be used by an operating system to determine what virtual memory location is needed so that the requested data can be brought into physical memory. The RTE instruction is then used to reload the processor's internal state at the time of the fault, the faulted bus cycle will then be re-run and the suspended instruction completed. If the faulted bus cycle was a read-modify-write, the entire cycle will be re-run whether the fault occurred during the read or the write operation.

An alternate method of handling a bus error is to complete the faulted access in software. In order to use this method, use of the special word, the instruction input buffer, the data input buffer, and the data output buffer image is required. The format of the special status word is shown in Figure 4-9. If the bus cycle was a write, the data output buffer image should be written to the fault address location using the function code contained in the special status word. If the cycle was a read, the data at the fault address location should be written to the images of the data input buffer, instruction input buffer, or both according to the DF and IF bits.* In addition, for read-modify-write cycles, the status register image must by properly set to reflect the read data if the fault occurred during the read portion of the cycle and the write operation (i.e., setting the most significant bit of the memory location) must also be performed. This is because the entire read-modify-write cycle is assumed to have been completed by software. Once the cycle has

---

*If the faulted access was a byte operation, the data should be moved from or to the least-significant byte of the data output or input buffer images unless the HB bit is set. This condition will only occur if a MOVEP instruction caused the fault during transfer of bits 8-15 of a word or long word or bits 24-31 of a long word.

been completed by software, the RR bit in the special status word is set to indicate to the processor that it should not re-run the cycle when the RTE instruction is executed. If the re-run flag is set when an RTE instruction executes, the MC68010 still reads all of the information from the stack.

15	14	13	12	11	10	9	8	7 - 3	2	1	0
RR	*	IF	DF	RM	HB	BY	RW	*		FC2-FC0	

RR — Re-run flag; 0 = processor re-run (default), 1 = software re-run.
IF — Instruction fetch to the Instruction Input Buffer.
DF — Data fetch to the Data Input Buffer.
RM — Read-Modify-Write cycle.
HB — High byte transfer from the Data Output Buffer or to the Data Input Buffer.
BY — Byte transfer flag; HB selects the high or low byte of the transfer register. If BY is clear, the transfer is word.
RW — Read/Write flag; 0 = write, 1 = read.
FC — The function code used during the faulted access.
* — These bits are reserved for future use by Motorola and will be zero when written by the MC68010.

Figure 4-9. Special Status Word Format

4.4.10 ADDRESS ERROR. Address error exceptions occur when the processor attempts to access a word or a long word operand or an instruction at an odd address. The effect is much like an internally generated bus error, so that the bus cycle is abortedd, ant processor ceases whatever processing it is currently doing and begins exception processing. After exception processing commences, the sequence is the same as that for bus error including the information that is stacked, except that the vector number refers to the address error vector instead. Likewise, if an address error occurs during the exception processing for a bus error, address error, or reset, the processor is halted.

On the MC68010, the address error exception stacks the same information that is stacked by a bus error exception, therefore it is possible to use the RTE instruction to continue execution of the suspended instruction. However, if the software re-run flag is not set, the fault address will be used when the cycle is re-run and another address error exception will occur. Therefore, the user must be certain that the proper corrections have been made to the stack image and user registers before attempting to continue the instruction. With proper software handling, the address error exception handler could emulate word or long word accesses to odd addresses if desired.

4.5 RETURN FROM EXCEPTION (MC68010)

In addition to returning from any exception handler routine on the MC68010, the RTE instruction is used to resume the execution of a suspended instruction by restoring all of the temporary register and control information stored during a bus error and returning to the normal processing state. For the RTE instruction to execute properly, the stack must contain valid and accessible data. The RTE instruction checks for data validity in two ways; first, by checking the format/offset word for a valid stack format code, and second, if the format code indicates the long stack format, the long stack data is checked for validity as it is loaded into the processor. In addition, the data is checked for accessibility when the processor starts reading the long data. Because of these checks, the RTE instruction executes as follows:

1 . Determine the stack format. This step is the same for any stack format and consists of reading the status register, program counter, and format/offset word. If the format code indicates a short stack format, execution continues at the new program counter address. If the format code is not one of the MC68010 defined stack format codes, exception processing starts for a format error.

2 . Determine data validity. For a long stack format, the MC68010 will begin to read the remaining stack data, checking for validity of the data. The only word checked for validity is the first of the 16 internal information words (SP + 26) shown in Figure 4-8. This word contains a processor version number in addition to proprietary internal information that must match the version number of the MC68010 that is attempting to read the data. This validity check is used to insure that in dual processor systems, the data will be properly interpreted by the RTE instruction if the two processors are of different versions. If the version number is incorrect for this processor, the RTE instruction will be aborted and exception processing will begin for a format error exception. Since the stack pointer is not updated until the RTE instruction has successfully read all of the stack data, a format error occurring at this point will not stack new data over the previous bus error stack information.

3 . Determine data accessibility. If the long stack data is valid, the MC68010 performs a read from the last word (SP + 56) of the long stack to determine data accessibility. If this read is terminated normally, the processor assumes that the remaining words on the stack frame are also accessible. If a bus error is signaled before or during this read, a bus error exception is taken as usual. After this read, the processor must be able to load the remaining data without receiving a bus error; therefore, if a bus error occurs on any of the remaining stack reads, the MC68010 treats this as a double bus fault and enters the halted state.

APPENDIX A
CONDITION CODES COMPUTATION

A.1 INTRODUCTION

This appendix provides a discussion of how the condition codes were developed, the meanings of each bit, how they are computed, and how they are represented in the instruction set details.

Two criteria were used in developing the condition codes:
- Consistency — across instruction, uses, and instances
- Meaningful Results — no change unless it provides useful information

The consistency across instructions means that instructions which are special cases of more general instructions affect the condition codes in the same way. Consistency across instances means that if an instruction ever affects a condition code, it will always affect that condition code. Consistency across uses means that whether the condition codes were set by a compare, test, or move instruction, the conditional instructions test the same situation. The tests used for the conditional instructions and the code computations are given in paragraph A.5.

A.2 CONDITION CODE REGISTER

The condition code register portion of the status register contains five bits:
- N — Negative
- Z — Zero
- V — Overflow
- C — Carry
- X — Extend

The first four bits are true condition code bits in that they reflect the condition of the result of a processor operation. The X bit is an operand for multiprecision computations. The carry bit (C) and the multiprecision operand extend bit (X) are separate in the MC68000 to simplify the programming model.

A.3 CONDITION CODE REGISTER NOTATION

In the instruction set details given in Appendix B, the description of the effect on the condition codes is given in the following form:

	X	N	Z	V	C

Condition Codes:

where:

N (negative)   Set if the most significant bit of the result is set. Cleared otherwise.

Z (zero)   Set if the result equals zero. Cleared otherwise.

V (overflow)   Set if there was an arithmetic overflow. This implies that the result is not representable in the operand size. Cleared otherwise.

C (carry)   Set if a carry is generated out of the most significant bit of the operands for an addition. Also set if a borrow is generated in a subtraction. Cleared otherwise.

X (extend)   Transparent to data movement. When affected, it is set the same as the C bit.

The notational convention that appears in the representation of the condition code register is:

*   set according to the result of the operation
—   not affected by the operation
0   cleared
1   set
U   undefined after the operation

A.4 CONDITION CODE COMPUTATION

Most operations take a source operand and a destination operand, compute, and store the result in the destination location. Unary operations take a destination operand, compute, and store the result in the destination location. Table A-1 details how each instruction sets the condition codes.

Table A-1. Condition Code Computations

Operations	X	N	Z	V	C	Special Definition
ABCD	*	U	?	U	?	$C = $ Decimal Carry $Z = Z \cdot \overline{Rm} \cdot \ldots \cdot \overline{R0}$
ADD, ADDI, ADDQ	*	*	*	?	?	$V = Sm \cdot Dm \cdot \overline{Rm} + \overline{Sm} \cdot \overline{Dm} \cdot Rm$ $C = Sm \cdot Dm + \overline{Rm} \cdot Dm + Sm \cdot \overline{Rm}$
ADDX	*	*	?	?	?	$V = Sm \cdot Dm \cdot \overline{Rm} + \overline{Sm} \cdot \overline{Dm} \cdot Rm$ $C = Sm \cdot Dm + Rm \cdot Dm + Sm \cdot \overline{Rm}$ $Z = Z \cdot \overline{Rm} \cdot \ldots \cdot \overline{R0}$
AND, ANDI, EOR, EORI, MOVEQ, MOVE, OR, ORI, CLR, EXT, NOT, TAS, TST	—	*	*	0	0	
CHK	—	*	U	U	U	
SUB, SUBI, SUBQ	*	*	*	?	?	$V = \overline{Sm} \cdot Dm \cdot \overline{Rm} + Sm \cdot \overline{Dm} \cdot Rm$ $C = Sm \cdot \overline{Dm} + Rm \cdot \overline{Dm} + Sm \cdot Rm$
SUBX	*	*	?	?	?	$V = \overline{Sm} \cdot Dm \cdot \overline{Rm} + Sm \cdot \overline{Dm} \cdot Rm$ $C = Sm \cdot \overline{Dm} + Rm \cdot \overline{Dm} + Sm \cdot Rm$ $Z = Z \cdot \overline{Rm} \cdot \ldots \cdot R0$
CMP, CMPI, CMPM	—	*	*	?	?	$V = \overline{Sm} \cdot Dm \cdot \overline{Rm} + Sm \cdot \overline{Dm} \cdot Rm$ $C = Sm \cdot \overline{Dm} + Rm \cdot \overline{Dm} + Sm \cdot Rm$
DIVS, DIVU	—	*	*	?	0	$V = $ Division Overflow
MULS, MULU	—	*	*	0	0	
SBCD, NBCD	*	U	?	U	?	$C = $ Decimal Borrow $Z = Z \cdot \overline{Rm} \cdot \ldots \cdot \overline{R0}$
NEG	*	*	*	?	?	$V = Dm \cdot Rm, \ C = Dm + Rm$
NEGX	*	*	?	?	?	$V = Dm \cdot Rm, \ C = Dm + Rm$ $Z = Z \cdot \overline{Rm} \cdot \ldots \cdot \overline{R0}$
BTST, BCHG, BSET, BCLR	—	—	?	—	—	$Z = \overline{Dn}$
ASL	*	*	*	?	?	$V = Dm \cdot (\overline{D_{m-1}} + \ldots + \overline{D_{m-r}})$ $\quad + \overline{Dm} \cdot (D_{m-1} + \ldots + D_{m-r})$ $C = D_{m-r+1}$
ASL (r=0)	—	*	*	0	0	
LSL, ROXL	*	*	*	0	?	$C = D_{m-r+1}$
LSR (r=0)	—	*	*	0	0	
ROXL (r=0)	—	*	*	0	?	$C = X$
ROL	—	*	*	0	?	$C = D_{m-r+1}$
ROL (r=0)	—	*	*	0	0	
ASR, LSR, ROXR	*	*	*	0	?	$C = D_{r-1}$
ASR, LSR (r=0)	—	*	*	0	0	
ROXR (r=0)	—	*	*	0	?	$C = X$
ROR	—	*	*	0	?	$C = D_{r-1}$
ROR (r=0)	—	*	*	0	0	

— Not affected
U Undefined
? Other — see Special Definition

*General Case:
$X = C$
$N = Rm$
$Z = Rm \cdot \ldots \cdot R0$

Sm Source Operand — most significant bit
Dm Destination operand — most significant bit
Rm Result operand — most significant bit
n bit number
r shift count

A.5 CONDITIONAL TESTS

Table A-2 lists the condition names, encodings, and tests for the conditional branch and set instructions. The test associated with each condition is a logical formula based on the current state of the condition codes. If this formula evaluates to 1, the condition succeeds, or is true. If the formula evaluates to 0, the condition is unsuccessful, or false. For example, the T condition always succeeds, while the EQ condition succeeds only if the Z bit is currently set in the condition codes.

Table A-2. Conditional Tests

Mnemonic	Condition	Encoding	Test
T	true	0000	1
F	false	0001	0
HI	high	0010	$\overline{C} \cdot \overline{Z}$
LS	low or same	0011	$C + Z$
CC (HS)	carry clear	0100	$\overline{C}$
CS (LO)	carry set	0101	C
NE	not equal	0110	$\overline{Z}$
EQ	equal	0111	Z
VC	overflow clear	1000	$\overline{V}$
VS	overflow set	1001	V
PL	plus	1010	$\overline{N}$
MI	minus	1011	N
GE	greater or equal	1100	$N \cdot V + \overline{N} \cdot \overline{V}$
LT	less than	1101	$N \cdot \overline{V} + \overline{N} \cdot V$
GT	greater than	1110	$N \cdot V \cdot \overline{Z} + \overline{N} \cdot \overline{V} \cdot \overline{Z}$
LE	less or equal	1111	$Z + N \cdot \overline{V} + \overline{N} \cdot V$

APPENDIX B
INSTRUCTION SET DETAILS

B.1 INTRODUCTION

This appendix contains detailed information about each instruction in the MC68000 instruction set. They are arranged in alphabetical order with the mnemonic heading set in large bold type for easy reference.

B.2 ADDRESSING CATEGORIES

Effective address modes may be categorized by the ways in which they may be used. The following classifications will be used in the instruction definitions.

Data | If an effective address mode may be used to refer to data operands, it is considered a data addressing effective address mode.

Memory | If an effective address mode may be used to refer to memory operands, it is considered a memory addressing effective address mode.

Alterable | If an effective address mode may be used to refer to alterable (writable) operands, it is considered an alterable addressing effective address mode.

Control | If an effective address mode may be used to refer to memory operands without an associated size, it is considered a control addressing effective address mode.

Table B-1 shows the various categories to which each of the effective address modes belong.

Table B-1. Effective Addressing Mode Categories

Addressing Mode	Mode	Register	Addressing Categories				Assembler Syntax
			Data	Memory	Control	Alterable	
Data Register Direct	000	reg. no.	X	—	—	X	Dn
Address Register Direct	001	reg. no.	—	—	—	X	An
Address Register Indirect	010	reg. no.	X	X	X	X	(An)
Address Register Indirect with Postincrement	011	reg. no.	X	X	—	X	(An)+
Address Register Indirect with Predecrement	100	reg. no.	X	X	—	X	−(An)
Address Register Indirect with Displacement	101	reg. no	X	X	X	X	d(An)
Address Register Indirect with Index	110	reg. no.	X	X	X	X	d(An, ix)
Absolute Short	111	000	X	X	X	X	xxx.W
Absolute Long	111	001	X	X	X	X	xxx.L
Program Counter with Displacement	111	010	X	X	X	—	d(PC)
Program Counter with Index	111	011	X	X	X	—	d(PC, ix)
Immediate	111	100	X	X	—	—	#xxx

These categories may be combined so that additional, more restrictive, classifications may be defined. For example, the instruction descriptions use such classifications as alterable memory or data alterable. The former refers to those addressing modes which are both alterable and memory addresses, and the latter refers to addressing modes which are both data and alterable.

B.3 INSTRUCTION DESCRIPTION

The formats of each instruction are given in the following pages. Figure B-1 illustrates what information is given.

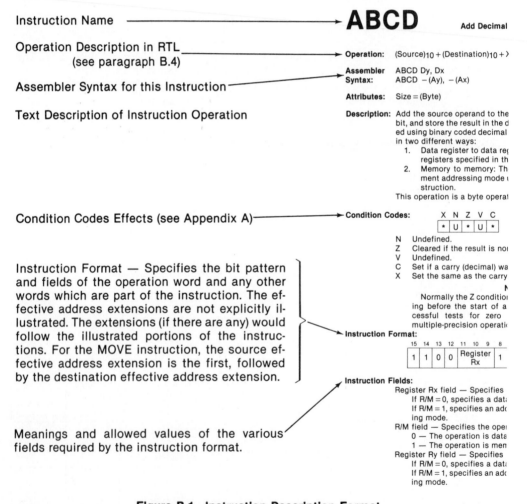

Figure B-1. Instruction Description Format

B.4 REGISTER TRANSFER LANGUAGE DEFINITIONS

The following register transfer language definitions are used for the operation description in the details of the instruction set.

OPERANDS:

An — address register
Dn — data register
Rn — any data or address register
PC — program counter
SR — status register
CCR — condition codes (low order byte of status register)

SSP — supervisor stack pointer
USP — user stack pointer
SP — active stack pointer (equivalent to A7)
X — extend operand (from condition codes)
Z — zero condition code
V — overflow condition code

Immediate Data — immediate data from the instruction
d — address displacement
Source — source effective address
Destination — destination effective address
Vector — location of exception vector

SUBFIELDS AND QUALIFIERS:

<bit>OF<operand>   selects a single bit of the operand
<operand>[<bit number>:<bit number>] selects a subfield of an operand
(<operand>)   the contents of the referenced location
<operand>₁₀   the operand is binary coded decimal; operations are to be performed in decimal.

(<address register>)   the register indirect operator which indicates that the operand re-
−(<address register>)   gister points to the memory location of the instruction operand. The
(<address register>)+   optional mode qualifiers are −, +, (d) and (d, ix); these are explained in Section 2.

OPERATIONS: Operations are grouped into binary, unary, and other.

Binary — These operations are written <operand><op><operand> where <op> is one of the following:
→   the left operand is moved to the location specified by the right operand
↔   the contents of the two operands are exchanged
+   the operands are added
−   the right operand is subtracted from the left operand
*   the operands are multiplied
/   the first operand is divided by the second operand
Λ   the operands are logically ANDed
v   the operands are logically ORed
⊕   the operands are logically exclusively ORed
<   relational test, true if left operand is less than right operand
>   relational test, true if left operand is not equal to right operand
shifted by   the left operand is shifted or rotated by the number of positions specified by the
rotated by   right operand

Unary:

~<operand>   the operand is logically complemented
<operand>sign-extended   the operand is sign extended, all bits of the upper half are made equal to high order bit of the lower half
<operand>tested   the operand is compared to 0, the results are used to set the condition codes

Other:

TRAP   equivalent to PC→(SSP)−; SR→(SSP)−; (vector)→PC
STOP   enter the stopped state, waiting for interrupts

If <condition> **then** <operations> **else** <operations>   The condition is tested. If true, the operations after the "then" are performed. If the condition is false and the optional "else" clause is present, the operations after the "else" are performed. If the condition is false and the optional "else" clause is absent, the instruction performs no operation.

ABCD   Add Decimal with Extend   ABCD

Operation: $(Source)_{10} + (Destination)_{10} + X \rightarrow Destination$

Assembler   ABCD Dy, Dx
Syntax: ABCD $-(Ay), -(Ax)$

Attributes: Size = (Byte)

Description: Add the source operand to the destination operand along with the extend bit, and store the result in the destination location. The addition is performed using binary coded decimal arithmetic. The operands may be addressed in two different ways:

1. Data register to data register: The operands are contained in the data registers specified in the instruction.
2. Memory to memory: The operands are addressed with the predecrement addressing mode using the address registers specified in the instruction.

This operation is a byte operation only.

Condition Codes:

X	N	Z	V	C
*	U	*	U	*

N   Undefined.
Z   Cleared if the result is non-zero. Unchanged otherwise.
V   Undefined.
C   Set if a carry (decimal) was generated. Cleared otherwise.
X   Set the same as the carry bit.

NOTE

Normally the Z condition code bit is set via programming before the start of an operation. This allows successful tests for zero results upon completion of multiple-precision operations.

Instruction Format:

15	14	13	12	11 10 9	8	7	6	5	4	3	2 1 0
1	1	0	0	Register Rx	1	0	0	0	0	R/M	Register Ry

Instruction Fields:

Register Rx field — Specifies the destination register:
If R/M = 0, specifies a data register.
If R/M = 1, specifies an address register for the predecrement addressing mode.

R/M field — Specifies the operand addressing mode:
0 — The operation is data register to data register.
1 — The operation is memory to memory.

Register Ry field — Specifies the source register:
If R/M = 0, specifies a data register.
If R/M = 1, specifies an address register for the predecrement addressing mode.

ADD

Add Binary

ADD

Operation: (Source) + (Destination) → Destination

Assembler ADD < ea >, Dn
Syntax: ADD Dn, < ea >

Attributes: Size = (Byte, Word, Long)

Description: Add the source operand to the destination operand, and store the result in the destination location. The size of the operation may be specified to be byte, word, or long. The mode of the instruction indicates which operand is the source and which is the destination as well as the operand size.

Condition Codes:

X	N	Z	V	C
*	*	*	*	*

N   Set if the result is negative. Cleared otherwise.
Z   Set if the result is zero. Cleared otherwise.
V   Set if an overflow is generated. Cleared otherwise.
C   Set if a carry is generated. Cleared otherwise.
X   Set the same as the carry bit.

Instruction Format:

15	14	13	12	11 10 9	8 7 6	5 4 3	2 1 0
1	1	0	1	Register	Op-Mode	Effective Address Mode	Register

Instruction Fields:

Register field — Specifies any of the eight data registers.
Op-Mode field —

Byte	Word	Long	Operation
000	001	010	(< Dn >) + (< ea >) → < Dn >
100	101	110	(< ea >) + (< Dn >) → < ea >

Effective Address field — Determines addressing mode:
a. If the location specified is a source operand, then all addressing modes are allowed as shown:

Addressing Mode	Mode	Register	Addressing Mode	Mode	Register
Dn	000	register number	d(An, Xi)	110	register number
An*	001	register number	Abs.W	111	000
(An)	010	register number	Abs.L	111	001
(An) +	011	register number	d(PC)	111	010
− (An)	100	register number	d(PC, Xi)	111	011
d(An)	101	register number	Imm	111	100

*Word and Long only.

— Continued —

Effective Address field (Continued)

b. If the location specified is a destination operand, then only alterable memory addressing modes are allowed as shown:

Addressing Mode	Mode	Register	Addressing Mode	Mode	Register
Dn	—	—	d(An, Xi)	110	register number
An	—	—	Abs.W	111	000
(An)	010	register number	Abs.L	111	001
(An) +	011	register number	d(PC)	—	—
− (An)	100	register number	d(PC, Xi)	—	—
d(An)	101	register number	Imm	—	—

Notes:

1. If the destination is a data register, then it cannot be specified by using the destination <ea> mode, but must use the destination Dn mode instead.
2. ADDA is used when the destination is an address register. ADDI and ADDQ are used when the source is immediate data. Most assemblers automatically make this distinction.

ADDA

Add Address

ADDA

Operation: (Source) + (Destination) → Destination

**Assembler
Syntax:** ADD < ea >, An

Attributes: Size = (Word, Long)

Description: Add the source operand to the destination address register, and store the result in the address register. The size of the operation may be specified to be word or long. The entire destination address register is used regardless of the operation size.

Condition Codes: Not affected.

Instruction Format:

15	14	13	12	11	10	9	8	7	6	5	4	3	2	1	0
1	1	0	1	Register			Op-Mode			Effective Address Mode			Register		

Instruction Fields:

Register field — Specifies any of the eight address registers. This is always the destination.

Op-Mode field — Specifies the size of the operation:

011 — word operation. The source operand is sign-extended to a long operand and the operation is performed on the address register using all 32 bits.

111 — long operation.

Effective Address field — Specifies the source operand. All addressing modes are allowed as shown:

Addressing Mode	Mode	Register	Addressing Mode	Mode	Register
Dn	000	register number	d(An, Xi)	110	register number
An	001	register number	Abs.W	111	000
(An)	010	register number	Abs.L	111	001
(An) +	011	register number	d(PC)	111	010
− (An)	100	register number	d(PC, Xi)	111	011
d(An)	101	register number	Imm	111	100

ADDI

Add Immediate

Operation: Immediate Data + (Destination) → Destination

**Assembler
Syntax:** ADDI #<data>,<ea>

Attributes: Size = (Byte, Word, Long)

Description: Add the immediate data to the destination operand, and store the result in the destination location. The size of the operation may be specified to be byte, word, or long. The size of the immediate data matches the operation size.

Condition Codes:

X	N	Z	V	C
*	*	*	*	*

N   Set if the result is negative. Cleared otherwise.
Z   Set if the result is zero. Cleared otherwise.
V   Set if an overflow is generated. Cleared otherwise.
C   Set if a carry is generated. Cleared otherwise.
X   Set the same as the carry bit.

Instruction Format:

15	14	13	12	11	10	9	8	7	6	5 4 3	2 1 0
0	0	0	0	0	1	1	0		Size	Effective Address Mode | Register	

Word Data (16 bits)	Byte Data (8 bits)

Long Data (32 bits, including previous word)

Instruction Fields:

Size field — Specifies the size of the operation:
00 — byte operation.
01 — word operation.
10 — long operation.

Effective Address field — Specifies the destination operand. Only data alterable addressing modes are allowed as shown:

Addressing Mode	Mode	Register	Addressing Mode	Mode	Register
Dn	000	register number	d(An, Xi)	110	register number
An	—	—	Abs.W	111	000
(An)	010	register number	Abs.L	111	001
(An)+	011	register number	d(PC)	—	—
−(An)	100	register number	d(PC, Xi)	—	—
d(An)	101	register number	Imm	—	—

Immediate field — (Data immediately following the instruction):
If size = 00, then the data is the low order byte of the immediate word.
If size = 01, then the data is the entire immediate word.
If size = 10, then the data is the next two immediate words.

ADDQ

ADDQ   Add Quick   **ADDQ**

Operation: Immediate Data + (Destination) → Destination

**Assembler
Syntax:** ADDQ #<data>, <ea>

Attributes: Size = (Byte, Word, Long)

Description: Add the immediate data to the operand at the destination location. The data range is from 1 to 8. The size of the operation may be specified to be byte, word, or long. Word and long operations are also allowed on the address registers and the condition codes are not affected. The entire destination address register is used regardless of the operation size.

Condition Codes:

X	N	Z	V	C
*	*	*	*	*

N   Set if the result is negative. Cleared otherwise.
Z   Set if the result is zero. Cleared otherwise.
V   Set if an overflow is generated. Cleared otherwise.
C   Set if a carry is generated. Cleared otherwise.
X   Set the same as the carry bit.

The condition codes are not affected if an addition to an address register is made.

Instruction Format:

15	14	13	12	11	10	9	8	7	6	5	4	3	2	1	0
0	1	0	1		Data		0		Size		Effective Address Mode			Register	

Instruction Fields:

Data field — Three bits of immediate data, 0, 1-7 representing a range of 8, 1 to 7 respectively.

Size field — Specifies the size of the operation:
00 — byte operation.
01 — word operation.
10 — long operation.

Effective Address field — Specifies the destination location. Only alterable addressing modes are allowed as shown:

Addressing Mode	Mode	Register	Addressing Mode	Mode	Register
Dn	000	register number	d(An, Xi)	110	register number
An*	001	register number	Abs.W	111	000
(An)	010	register number	Abs.L	111	001
(An) +	011	register number	d(PC)	—	—
− (An)	100	register number	d(PC, Xi)	—	—
d(An)	101	register number	Imm	—	—

*Word and Long only.

ADDX   Add Extended   # ADDX

Operation: (Source) + (Destination) + X → Destination

Assembler   ADDX Dy, Dx
Syntax: ADDX − (Ay), − (Ax)

Attributes: Size = (Byte, Word, Long)

Description: Add the source operand to the destination operand along with the extend bit and store the result in the destination location. The operands may be addressed in two different ways:

1. Data register to data register: the operands are contained in data registers specified in the instruction.
2. Memory to memory: the operands are addressed with the predecrement addressing mode using the address registers specified in the instruction.

The size of the operation may be specified to be byte, word, or long.

Condition Codes:

X	N	Z	V	C
*	*	*	*	*

N   Set if the result is negative. Cleared otherwise.
Z   Cleared if the result is non-zero. Unchanged otherwise.
V   Set if an overflow is generated. Cleared otherwise.
C   Set if a carry is generated. Cleared otherwise.
X   Set the same as the carry bit.

NOTE

Normally the Z condition code bit is set via programming before the start of an operation. This allows successful tests for zero results upon completion of multiple-precision operations.

Instruction Format:

15	14	13	12	11	10	9	8	7	6	5	4	3	2	1	0
1	1	0	1	Register Rx			1	Size		0	0	R/M	Register Ry		

Instruction Fields:

Register Rx field — Specifies the destination register:
   If R/M = 0, specifies a data register.
   If R/M = 1, specifies an address register for the predecrement addressing mode.

Size field — Specifies the size of the operation:
   00 — byte operation.
   01 — word operation.
   10 — long operation.

— Continued —

ADDX

Add Extended

ADDX

Instruction Fields: (Continued)

R/M field — Specifies the operand addressing mode:

0 — The operation is data register to data register.

1 — The operation is memory to memory.

Register Ry field — Specifies the source register:

If R/M = 0, specifies a data register.

If R/M = 1, specifies an address register for the predecrement addressing mode.

AND

AND Logical

Operation: (Source)Λ(Destination) → Destination

Assembler AND <ea>, Dn
Syntax: AND Dn, <ea>

Attributes: Size = (Byte, Word, Long)

Description: AND the source operand to the destination operand and store the result in the destination location. The size of the operation may be specified to be byte, word, or long. The contents of an address register may not be used as an operand.

Condition Codes:

X	N	Z	V	C
—	*	*	0	0

N   Set if the most significant bit of the result is set. Cleared otherwise.
Z   Set if the result is zero. Cleared otherwise.
V   Always cleared.
C   Always cleared.
X   Not affected.

Instruction Format:

15	14	13	12	11 10 9	8 7 6	5 4 3	2 1 0
1	1	0	0	Register	Op-Mode	Effective Address Mode	Register

Instruction Fields:

Register field — Specifies any of the eight data registers.
Op-Mode field —

Byte	Word	Long	Operation
000	001	010	(<Dn>) Λ (<ea>) → <Dn>
100	101	110	(<ea>) Λ (<Dn>) → <ea>

Effective Address field — Determines addressing mode:
If the location specified is a source operand then only data addressing modes are allowed as shown:

Addressing Mode	Mode	Register	Addressing Mode	Mode	Register
Dn	000	register number	d(An, Xi)	110	register number
An	—	—	Abs.W	111	000
(An)	010	register number	Abs.L	111	001
(An)+	011	register number	d(PC)	111	010
−(An)	100	register number	d(PC, Xi)	111	011
d(An)	101	register number	Imm	111	100

— Continued —

AND

AND

Effective Address field (Continued)

If the location specified is a destination operand then only alterable memory addressing modes are allowed as shown:

Addressing Mode	Mode	Register	Addressing Mode	Mode	Register
Dn	—	—	d(An, Xi)	110	register number
An	—	—	Abs.W	111	000
(An)	010	register number	Abs.L	111	001
(An)+	011	register number	d(PC)	—	—
−(An)	100	register number	d(PC, Xi)	—	—
d(An)	101	register number	Imm	—	—

Notes: 1.   If the destination is a data register, then it cannot be specified by using the destination <ea> mode, but must use the destination Dn mode instead.

2.   ANDI is used when the source is immediate data. Most assemblers automatically make this distinction.

ANDI

AND Immediate

ANDI

Operation: Immediate Data Λ (Destination)→ Destination

**Assembler
Syntax:** ANDI #<data>, <ea>

Attributes: Size = (Byte, Word, Long)

Description: AND the immediate data to the destination operand and store the result in the destination location. The size of the operation may be specified to be byte, word, or long. The size of the immediate data matches the operation size.

Condition Codes:

X	N	Z	V	C
—	*	*	0	0

N Set if the most significant bit of the result is set. Cleared otherwise.
Z Set if the result is zero. Cleared otherwise.
V Always cleared.
C Always cleared.
X Not affected.

Instruction Format:

15	14	13	12	11	10	9	8	7	6	5	4	3	2	1	0
0	0	0	0	0	0	1	0	Size		Effective Address Mode | Register					
Word Data (16 bits)								Byte Data (8 bits)							
Long Data (32 bits, including previous word)															

Instruction Fields:

Size field — Specifies the size of the operation:
00 — byte operation.
01 — word operation.
10 — long operation.

Effective Address field — Specifies the destination operand. Only data alterable addressing modes are allowed as shown:

Addressing Mode	Mode	Register	Addressing Mode	Mode	Register
Dn	000	register number	d(An, Xi)	110	register number
An	—	—	Abs.W	111	000
(An)	010	register number	Abs.L	111	001
(An) +	011	register number	d(PC)	—	—
− (An)	100	register number	d(PC, Xi)	—	—
d(An)	101	register number	Imm	—	—

Immediate field — (Data immediately following the instruction):
If size = 00, then the data is the low order byte of the immediate word.
If size = 01, then the data is the entire immediate word.
If size = 10, then the data is the next two immediate words.

ANDI
to CCR

ANDI
to CCR

Operation: $(Source) \wedge CCR \rightarrow CCR$

Assembler
Syntax: ANDI #xxx, CCR

Attributes: Size = (Byte)

Description: AND the immediate operand with the condition codes and store the result in the low-order byte of the status register.

Condition Codes:

X	N	Z	V	C
*	*	*	*	*

N   Cleared if bit 3 of immediate operand is zero. Unchanged otherwise.
Z   Cleared if bit 2 of immediate operand is zero. Unchanged otherwise.
V   Cleared if bit 1 of immediate operand is zero. Unchanged otherwise.
C   Cleared if bit 0 of immediate operand is zero. Unchanged otherwise.
X   Cleared if bit 4 of immediate operand is zero. Unchanged otherwise.

Instruction Format:

15	14	13	12	11	10	9	8	7	6	5	4	3	2	1	0
0	0	0	0	0	0	1	0	0	0	1	1	1	1	0	0
0	0	0	0	0	0	0	0	Byte Data (8 bits)							

ANDI
to SR

AND Immediate to the Status Register
(Privileged Instruction)

ANDI
to SR

Operation: If supervisor state
then (Source)ΛSR → SR
else TRAP

Assembler
Syntax: ANDI #xxx, SR

Attributes: Size = (Word)

Description: AND the immediate operand with the contents of the status register and store the result in the status register. All bits of the status register are affected.

Condition Codes:

X	N	Z	V	C
*	*	*	*	*

N   Cleared if bit 3 of immediate operand is zero. Unchanged otherwise.
Z   Cleared if bit 2 of immediate operand is zero. Unchanged otherwise.
V   Cleared if bit 1 of immediate operand is zero. Unchanged otherwise.
C   Cleared if bit 0 of immediate operand is zero. Unchanged otherwise.
X   Cleared if bit 4 of immediate operand is zero. Unchanged otherwise.

Instruction Format:

15	14	13	12	11	10	9	8	7	6	5	4	3	2	1	0
0	0	0	0	0	0	1	0	0	1	1	1	1	1	0	0
Word Data (16 bits)															

ASL, ASR Arithmetic Shift ASL, ASR

Operation: (Destination) Shifted by <count> → Destination

Assembler Syntax:
ASd Dx, Dy
ASd #<data>, Dy
ASd <ea>

Attributes: Size = (Byte, Word, Long)

Description: Arithmetically shift the bits of the operand in the direction specified. The carry bit receives the last bit shifted out of the operand. The shift count for the shifting of a register may be specified in two different ways:
1. Immediate: the shift count is specified in the instruction (shift range, 1-8).
2. Register: the shift count is contained in a data register specified in the instruction.

The size of the operation may be specified to be byte, word, or long. The content of memory may be shifted one bit only and the operand size is restricted to a word.

For ASL, the operand is shifted left; the number of positions shifted is the shift count. Bits shifted out of the high order bit go to both the carry and the extend bits; zeroes are shifted into the low order bit. The overflow bit indicates if any sign changes occur during the shift.

ASL:

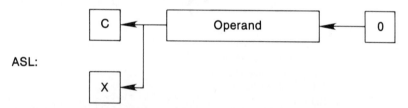

For ASR, the operand is shifted right; the number of positions shifted is the shift count. Bits shifted out of the low order bit go to both the carry and the extend bits; the sign bit is replicated into the high order bit.

ASR:

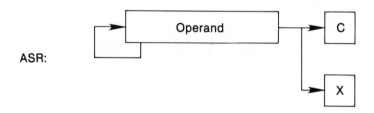

— Continued —

ASL, ASR   <small>Arithmetic Shift</small>   ASL, ASR

Condition Codes:

X	N	Z	V	C
*	*	*	*	*

N   Set if the most significant bit of the result is set. Cleared otherwise.

Z   Set if the result is zero. Cleared otherwise.

V   Set if the most significant bit is changed at any time during the shift operation. Cleared otherwise.

C   Set according to the last bit shifted out of the operand. Cleared for a shift count of zero.

X   Set according to the last bit shifted out of the operand. Unaffected for a shift count of zero.

Instruction Format (Register Shifts):

15	14	13	12	11	10	9	8	7	6	5	4	3	2	1	0
1	1	1	0	Count/Register			dr	Size		i/r	0	0	Register		

Instruction Fields (Register Shifts):

Count/Register field — Specifies shift count or register where count is located:

If i/r = 0, the shift count is specified in this field. The values 0, 1-7 represent a range of 8, 1 to 7 respectively.

If i/r = 1, the shift count (modulo 64) is contained in the data register specified in this field.

dr field — Specifies the direction of the shift:

0 — shift right.

1 — shift left.

Size field — Specifies the size of the operation:

00 — byte operation.

01 — word operation.

10 — long operation.

i/r field —

If i/r = 0, specifies immediate shift count.

if i/r = 1, specifies register shift count.

Register field — Specifies a data register whose content is to be shifted.

Instruction Format (Memory Shifts):

15	14	13	12	11	10	9	8	7	6	5	4	3	2	1	0
1	1	1	0	0	0	0	dr	1	1	Effective Address Mode			Register		

— Continued —

ASL, ASR   Arithmetic Shift   ASL, ASR

Instruction Fields (Memory Shifts):

dr field — Specifies the direction of the shift:

0 — shift right.

1 — shift left.

Effective Address field — Specifies the operand to be shifted. Only memory alterable addressing modes are allowed as shown:

Addressing Mode	Mode	Register	Addressing Mode	Mode	Register
Dn	—	—	d(An, Xi)	110	register number
An	—	—	Abs.W	111	000
(An)	010	register number	Abs.L	111	001
(An)+	011	register number	d(PC)	—	—
–(An)	100	register number	d(PC, Xi)	—	—
d(An)	101	register number	Imm	—	—

Bcc

Branch Conditionally

Bcc

Operation: If (condition true) then PC + d → PC

**Assembler
Syntax:** Bcc < label >

Attributes: Size = (Byte, Word)

Description: If the specified condition is met, program execution continues at location (PC) + displacement. Displacement is a twos complement integer which counts the relative distance in bytes. The value in PC is the current instruction location plus two. If the 8-bit displacement in the instruction word is zero, then the 16-bit displacement (word immediately following the instruction) is used. "cc" may specify the following conditions:

CC	carry clear	0100	$\overline{C}$	LS	low or same	0011	$C + Z$	
CS	carry set	0101	C	LT	less than	1101	$N \cdot \overline{V} + \overline{N} \cdot V$	
EQ	equal	0111	Z	MI	minus	1011	N	
GE	greater or equal	1100	$N \cdot V + \overline{N} \cdot \overline{V}$	NE	not equal	0110	$\overline{Z}$	
GT	greater than	1110	$N \cdot V \cdot \overline{Z} + \overline{N} \cdot \overline{V} \cdot \overline{Z}$	PL	plus	1010	$\overline{N}$	
HI	high	0010	$\overline{C} \cdot \overline{Z}$	VC	overflow clear	1000	$\overline{V}$	
LE	less or equal	1111	$Z + N \cdot \overline{V} + \overline{N} \cdot V$	VS	overflow set	1001	V	

Condition Codes: Not affected.

Instruction Format:

15	14	13	12	11	10	9	8	7	6	5	4	3	2	1	0
0	1	1	0	Condition				8-bit Displacement							
16-bit Displacement if 8-bit Displacement = 0															

Instruction Fields:

Condition field — One of fourteen conditions discussed in description.

8-bit Displacement field — Twos complement integer specifying the relative distance (in bytes) between the branch instruction and the next instruction to be executed if the condition is met.

16-bit Displacement field — Allows a larger displacement than 8 bits. Used only if the 8-bit displacement is equal to zero.

Note: A short branch to the immediately following instruction cannot be done because it would result in a zero offset which forces a word branch instruction definition.

BCHG

Test a Bit and Change

BCHG

Operation: ~(<bit number>) OF Destination → Z;
~(<bit number>) OF Destination → <bit number> OF Destination

Assembler BCHG Dn, <ea>
Syntax: BCHG #<data>, <ea>

Attributes: Size = (Byte, Long)

Description: A bit in the destination operand is tested and the state of the specified bit is reflected in the Z condition code. After the test, the state of the specified bit is changed in the destination. If a data register is the destination, then the bit numbering is modulo 32 allowing bit manipulation on all bits in a data register. If a memory location is the destination, a byte is read from that location, the bit operation performed using the bit number modulo 8, and the byte written back to the location with zero referring to the least-significant bit. The bit number for this operation may be specified in two different ways:
1. Immediate — the bit number is specified in a second word of the instruction.
2. Register — the bit number is contained in a data register specified in the instruction.

Condition Codes:

X	N	Z	V	C
—	—	*	—	—

N Not affected.
Z Set if the bit tested is zero. Cleared otherwise.
V Not affected.
C Not affected.
X Not affected.

Instruction Format (Bit Number Dynamic):

15	14	13	12	11	10	9	8	7	6	5	4	3	2	1	0
0	0	0	0	Register			1	0	1	Effective Address Mode			Register		

Instruction Fields (Bit Number Dynamic):

Register field — Specifies the data register whose content is the bit number.

Effective Address field — Specifies the destination location. Only data alterable addressing modes are allowed as shown:

Addressing Mode	Mode	Register	Addressing Mode	Mode	Register
Dn*	000	register number	d(An, Xi)	110	register number
An	—	—	Abs.W	111	000
(An)	010	register number	Abs.L	111	001
(An)+	011	register number	d(PC)	—	—
−(An)	100	register number	d(PC, Xi)	—	—
d(An)	101	register number	Imm	—	—

*Long only; all others are byte only.

— Continued —

BCHG

Test a Bit and Change

BCHG

Instruction Format (Bit Number Static):

	15	14	13	12	11	10	9	8	7	6	5 4 3	2 1 0
	0	0	0	0	1	0	0	0	0	1	Effective Address	
											Mode	Register
	0	0	0	0	0	0	0	0			bit number	

Instruction Fields (Bit Number Static):

Effective Address field — Specifies the destination location. Only data alterable addressing modes are allowed as shown:

Addressing Mode	Mode	Register	Addressing Mode	Mode	Register
Dn	000	register number	d(An, Xi)	110	register number
An	—	—	Abs.W	111	000
(An)	010	register number	Abs.L	111	001
(An)+	011	register number	d(PC)	—	—
−(An)	100	register number	d(PC, Xi)	—	—
d(An)	101	register number	Imm	—	—

*Long only; all others are byte only.

bit number field — Specifies the bit numbers.

BCLR

Test a Bit and Clear

BCLR

Operation: ~(<bit number>) OF Destination)→Z;
0→<bit number> OF Destination

Assembler BLCR Dn, <ea>
Syntax: BCLR #<data>, <ea>

Attributes: Size = (Byte, Long)

Description: A bit in the destination operand is tested and the state of the specified bit is reflected in the Z condition code. After the test, the specified bit is cleared in the destination. If a data register is the destination, then the bit numbering is modulo 32 allowing bit manipulation on all bits in a data register. If a memory location is the destination, a byte is read from that location, the bit operation performed using the bit number modulo 8, and the byte written back to the location with zero referring to the least-significant bit. The bit number for this operation may be specified in two different ways:

1. Immediate — the bit number is specified in a second word of the instruction.
2. Register — the bit number is contained in a data register specified in the instruction.

Condition Codes:

X	N	Z	V	C
—	—	*	—	—

N Not affected.
Z Set if the bit tested is zero. Cleared otherwise.
V Not affected.
C Not affected.
X Not affected.

Instruction Format (Bit Number Dynamic):

15	14	13	12	11	10	9	8	7	6	5	4	3	2	1	0
0	0	0	0	Register			1	1	0	Effective Address Mode | Register					

Instruction Fields (Bit Number Dynamic):

Register field — Specifies the data register whose content is the bit number.

Effective Address field — Specifies the destination location. Only data alterable addressing modes are allowed as shown:

Addressing Mode	Mode	Register	Addressing Mode	Mode	Register
Dn*	000	register number	d(An, Xi)	110	register number
An	—	—	Abs.W	111	000
(An)	010	register number	Abs.L	111	001
(An) +	011	register number	d(PC)	—	—
– (An)	100	register number	d(PC, Xi)	—	—
d(An)	101	register number	Imm	—	—

*Long only; all others are byte only.

— Continued —

BCLR

Test a Bit and Clear

BCLR

Instruction Format (Bit Number Static):

15	14	13	12	11	10	9	8	7	6	5 4 3	2 1 0
0	0	0	0	1	0	0	0	1	0	Effective Address Mode	Register
0	0	0	0	0	0	0	0			bit number	

Instruction Fields (Bit Number Static):

Effective Address field — Specifies the destination location. Only data alterable addressing modes are allowed as shown:

Addressing Mode	Mode	Register	Addressing Mode	Mode	Register
Dn*	000	register only	d(An, Xi)	110	register number
An	—	—	Abs.W	111	000
(An)	010	register number	Abs.L	111	001
(An)+	011	register number	d(PC)	—	—
−(An)	100	register number	d(PC, Xi)	—	—
d(An)	101	register number	Imm	—	—

*Long only; all others are byte only.

bit number field — Specifies the bit number.

BRA

Branch Always

BRA

Operation: PC + d → PC

**Assembler
Syntax:** BRA < label >

Attributes: Size = (Byte, Word)

Description: Program execution continues at location (PC) + displacement. Displacement is a twos complement integer which counts the relative distance in bytes. The value in PC is the current instruction location plus two. If the 8-bit displacement in the instruction word is zero, then the 16-bit displacement (word immediately following the instruction) is used.

Condition Codes: Not affected.

Instruction Format:

15	14	13	12	11	10	9	8	7	6	5	4	3	2	1	0
0	1	1	0	0	0	0	0				8-bit Displacement				
16-bit Displacement if 8-bit Displacement = 0															

Instruction Fields:

8-bit Displacement field — Twos complement integer specifying the relative distance (in bytes) between the branch instruction and the next instruction to be executed if the condition is met.

16-bit Displacement field — Allows a larger displacement than 8 bits. Used only if the 8-bit displacement is equal to zero.

Note: A short branch to the immediately following instruction cannot be done because it would result in a zero offset which forces a word branch instruction definition.

BSET

Test a Bit and Set

BSET

Operation: ~(<bit number>) OF Destination → Z
1 → <bit number> OF Destination

Assembler BSET Dn, <ea>
Syntax: BSET #<data>, <ea>

Attributes: Size = (Byte, Long)

Description: A bit in the destination operand is tested and the state of the specified bit is reflected in the Z condition code. After the test, the specified bit is set in the destination. If a data register is the destination, then the bit numbering is modulo 32, allowing bit manipulation on all bits in a data register. If a memory location is the destination, a byte is read from that location, the bit operation performed using the bit number modulo 8, and the byte written back to the location with zero referring to the least-significant bit. The bit number for this operation may be specified in two different ways:

1. Immediate — the bit number is specified in a second word of the instruction.
2. Register — the bit number is contained in a data register specified in the instruction.

Condition Codes:

X	N	Z	V	C
—	—	*	—	—

N   Not affected.
Z   Set if the bit tested is zero. Cleared otherwise.
V   Not affected.
C   Not affected.
X   Not affected.

Instruction Format (Bit Number Dynamic):

15	14	13	12	11	10	9	8	7	6	5	4	3	2	1	0
0	0	0	0	Register			1	1	1	Effective Address Mode | Register					

Instruction Fields (Bit Number Dynamic):
Register field — Specifies the data register whose content is the bit number.
Effective Address field — Specifies the destination location. Only data alterable addressing modes are allowed as shown:

Addressing Mode	Mode	Register	Addressing Mode	Mode	Register
Dn*	000	register number	d(An, Xi)	110	register number
An	—	—	Abs.W	111	000
(An)	010	register number	Abs.L	111	001
(An) +	011	register number	d(PC)	—	—
− (An)	100	register number	d(PC, Xi)	—	—
d(An)	101	register number	Imm	—	—

*Long only; all others are byte only

— Continued —

BSET

Test a Bit and Set

BSET

Instruction Format (Bit Number Static):

15	14	13	12	11	10	9	8	7	6	5 4 3	2 1 0
0	0	0	0	1	0	0	0	1	1	Effective Address Mode	Register
0	0	0	0	0	0	0	0			bit number	

Instruction Fields (Bit Number Static):

Effective Address field — Specifies the destination location. Only data alterable addressing modes are allowed as shown:

Addressing Mode	Mode	Register	Addressing Mode	Mode	Register
Dn*	000	register number	d(An, Xi)	110	register number
An	—	—	Abs.W	111	000
(An)	010	register number	Abs.L	111	001
(An)+	011	register number	d(PC)	—	—
−(An)	100	register number	d(PC, Xi)	—	—
d(An)	101	register number	Imm	—	—

*Long only; all others are byte only.

bit number field — Specifies the bit number.

BSR

Branch to Subroutine

BSR

Operation: PC $\rightarrow$ – (SP); PC + d $\rightarrow$ PC

Assembler
Syntax: BSR < label >

Attributes: Size = (Byte, Word)

Description: The long word address of the instruction immediately following the BSR instruction is pushed onto the system stack. Program execution then continues at location (PC) + displacement. Displacement is a twos complement integer which counts the relative distances in bytes. The value in PC is the current instruction location plus two. If the 8-bit displacement in the instruction word is zero, then the 16-bit displacement (word immediately following the instruction) is used.

Condition Codes: Not affected.

Instruction Format:

15	14	13	12	11	10	9	8	7	6	5	4	3	2	1	0
0	1	1	0	0	0	0	1	8-bit Displacement							
16-bit Displacement if 8-bit Displacement = 0															

Instruction Fields:

8-bit Displacement field — Twos complement integer specifying the relative distance (in bytes) between the branch instruction and the next instruction to be executed if the condition is met.

16-bit Displacement field — Allows a larger displacement than 8 bits. Used only if the 8-bit displacement is equal to zero.

Note: A short subroutine branch to the immediately following instruction cannot be done because it would result in a zero offset which forces a word branch instruction definition.

BTST

Test a Bit

BTST

Operation: ~(<bit number>) OF Destination→Z

Assembler BTST Dn, <ea>
Syntax: BTST #<data>, <ea>

Attributes: Size = (Byte, Long)

Description: A bit in the destination operand is tested and the state of the specified bit is reflected in the Z condition code. If a data register is the destination, then the bit numbering is modulo 32, allowing bit manipulation on all bits in a data register. If a memory location is the destination, a byte is read from that location, and the bit operation performed using the bit number modulo 8 with zero referring to the least-signifcant bit. The bit number for this operation may be specified in two different ways:

1. Immediate — the bit number is specified in a second word of the instruction.
2. Register — the bit number is contained in a data register specified in the instruction.

Condition Codes:

X	N	Z	V	C
—	—	*	—	—

N   Not affected.
Z   Set if the bit tested is zero. Cleared otherwise.
V   Not affected.
C   Not affected.
X   Not affected.

Instruction Format (Bit Number Dynamic):

15	14	13	12	11	10	9	8	7	6	5	4	3	2	1	0
0	0	0	0	Register			1	0	0	Effective Address Mode | Register					

Instruction Fields (Bit Number Dynamic):

Register field — Specifies the data register whose content is the bit number.

Effective Address field — Specifies the destination location. Only data addressing modes are allowed as shown:

Addressing Mode	Mode	Register	Addressing Mode	Mode	Register
Dn*	000	register number	d(An, Xi)	110	register number
An	—	—	Abs.W	111	000
(An)	010	register number	Abs.L	111	001
(An)+	011	register number	d(PC)	111	010
−(An)	100	register number	d(PC, Xi)	111	011
d(An)	101	register number	Imm	111	100

*Long only; all others are byte only.

— Continued —

BTST

BTST

Test a Bit

Instruction Format (Bit Number Static):

15	14	13	12	11	10	9	8	7	6	5 4 3	2 1 0
0	0	0	0	1	0	0	0	0	0	Effective Address Mode	Register
0	0	0	0	0	0	0	0			bit number	

Instruction Fields (Bit Number Static):

Effective Address field — Specifies the destination location. Only data addressing modes are allowed as shown:

Addressing Mode	Mode	Register	Addressing Mode	Mode	Register
Dn*	000	register number	d(An, Xi)	110	register number
An	—	—	Abs.W	111	000
(An)	010	register number	Abs.L	111	001
(An) +	011	register number	d(PC)	111	010
− (An)	100	register number	d(PC, Xi)	111	011
d(An)	101	register number	Imm	—	—

*Long only; all others are byte only.

bit number field — Specifies the bit number.

CHK

Check Register Against Bounds

Operation: If Dn<0 or Dn> (<ea>) then TRAP

**Assembler
Syntax:**   CHK <ea>, Dn

Attributes: Size = (Word)

Description: The content of the low order word in the data register specified in the instruction is examined and compared to the upper bound. The upper bound
is a twos complement integer. If the register value is less than zero or
greater than the upper bound contained in the operand word, then the processor initiates exception processing. The vector number is generated to
reference the CHK instruction exception vector.

Condition Codes:

X	N	Z	V	C
—	*	U	U	U

N   Set if Dn<0; cleared if Dn> (<ea>). Undefined otherwise.
Z   Undefined.
V   Undefined.
C   Undefined.
X   Not affected.

Instruction Format:

15	14	13	12	11	10	9	8	7	6	5	4	3	2	1	0
0	1	0	0	Register			1	1	0	Effective Address					
										Mode			Register		

Instruction Fields:

Register field — Specifies the data register whose content is checked.
Effective Address field — Specifies the upper bound operand word. Only
data addressing modes are allowed as shown:

Addressing Mode	Mode	Register	Addressing Mode	Mode	Register
Dn	000	register number	d(An, Xi)	110	register number
An	—	—	Abs.W	111	000
(An)	010	register number	Abs.L	111	001
(An)+	011	register number	d(PC)	111	010
−(An)	100	register number	d(PC, Xi)	111	011
d(An)	101	register number	Imm	111	100

CLR

Clear an Operand

CLR

Operation: 0 → Destination

**Assembler
Syntax:**   CLR < ea >

Attributes: Size = (Byte, Word, Long)

Description: The destination is cleared to all zero bits. The size of the operation may be specified to be byte, word, or long.

Condition Codes:

X	N	Z	V	C
—	0	1	0	0

N   Always cleared.
Z   Always set.
V   Always cleared.
C   Always cleared.
X   Not affected.

Instruction Format:

15	14	13	12	11	10	9	8	7	6	5 4 3	2 1 0
0	1	0	0	0	0	1	0	Size		Effective Address Mode	Register

Instruction Fields:

Size field — Specifies the size of the operation:
00 — byte operation.
01 — word operation.
10 — long operation.

Effective Address field — Specifies the destination location. Only data alterable addressing modes are allowed as shown:

Addressing Mode	Mode	Register	Addressing Mode	Mode	Register
Dn	000	register number	d(An, Xi)	110	register number
An	—	—	Abs.W	111	000
(An)	010	register number	Abs.L	111	001
(An) +	011	register number	d(PC)	—	—
− (An)	100	register number	d(PC, Xi)	—	—
d(An)	101	register number	Imm	—	—

Note: A memory destination is read before it is written to.

CMP

Compare

CMP

Operation: (Destination) − (Source)

**Assembler
Syntax:** CMP <ea>, Dn

Attributes: Size = (Byte, Word, Long)

Description: Subtract the source operand from the destination operand and set the condition codes according to the result; the destination location is not changed. The size of the operation may be specified to be byte, word, or long.

Condition Codes:

X	N	Z	V	C
—	*	*	*	*

N Set if the result is negative. Cleared otherwise.
Z Set if the result is zero. Cleared otherwise.
V Set if an overflow is generated. Cleared otherwise.
C Set if a borrow is generated. Cleared otherwise.
X Not affected.

Instruction Format:

15	14	13	12	11 10 9	8 7 6	5 4 3	2 1 0
1	0	1	1	Register	Op-Mode	Effective Address Mode	Register

Instruction Fields:

Register field — Specifies the destination data register.
Op-Mode field —

Byte	Word	Long	Operation
000	001	010	(<Dn>) − (<ea>)

Effective Address field — Specifies the source operand. All addressing modes are allowed as shown:

Addressing Mode	Mode	Register	Addressing Mode	Mode	Register
Dn	000	register number	d(An, Xi)	110	register number
An*	001	register number	Abs.W	111	000
(An)	010	register number	Abs.L	111	001
(An) +	011	register number	d(PC)	111	010
− (An)	100	register number	d(PC, Xi)	111	011
d(An)	101	register number	Imm	111	100

*Word and Long only.

Note: CMPA is used when the destination is an address register. CMPI is used when the source is immediate data. CMPM is used for memory to memory compares. Most assemblers automatically make this distinction.

CMPA

Compare Address

CMPA

Operation: (Destination) – (Source)

**Assembler
Syntax:** CMPA <ea>, An

Attributes: Size = (Word, Long)

Description: Subtract the source operand from the destination address register and set the condition codes according to the result; the address register is not changed. The size of the operation may be specified to be word or long. Word length source operands are sign extended to 32 bit quantities before the operation is done.

Condition Code:

X	N	Z	V	C
—	*	*	*	*

N   Set if the result is negative. Cleared otherwise.
Z   Set if the result is zero. Cleared otherwise.
V   Set if an overflow is generated. Cleared otherwise.
C   Set if a borrow is generated. Cleared otherwise.
X   Not affected.

Instruction Format:

15	14	13	12	11 10 9	8 7 6	5 4 3	2 1 0
1	0	1	1	Register	Op-Mode	Effective Address Mode	Register

Instruction Fields:

Register field — Specifies the destination address register.

Op-Mode field — Specifies the size of the operation:

011 — word operation. The source operand is sign-extended to a long operand and the operation is performed on the address register using all 32 bits.

111 — long operation.

Effective Address field — Specifies the source operand. All addressing modes are allowed as shown:

Addressing Mode	Mode	Register	Addressing Mode	Mode	Register
Dn	000	register number	d(An, Xi)	110	register number
An	001	register number	Abs.W	111	000
(An)	010	register number	Abs.L	111	001
(An)+	011	register number	d(PC)	111	010
– (An)	100	register number	d(PC, Xi)	111	011
d(An)	101	register number	Imm	111	100

CMPI

Compare Immediate

CMPI

Operation: (Destination) – Immediate Data

**Assembler
Syntax:**   CMPI #<data>, <ea>

Attributes: Size = (Byte, Word, Long)

Description: Subtract the immediate data from the destination operand and set the condition codes according to the result; the destination location is not changed. The size of the operation may be specified to be byte, word, or long. The size of the immediate data matches the operation size.

Condition Codes:

X	N	Z	V	C
—	*	*	*	*

N   Set if the result is negative. Cleared otherwise.
Z   Set if the result is zero. Cleared otherwise.
V   Set if an overflow is generated. Cleared otherwise.
C   Set if a borrow is generated. Cleared otherwise.
X   Not affected.

Instruction Format:

15	14	13	12	11	10	9	8	7	6	5	4	3	2	1	0
0	0	0	0	1	1	0	0	Size		Effective Address Mode | Register					
Word Data (16 bits)								Byte Data (8 bits)							
Long Data (32 bits, including previous word)															

Instruction Fields:

Size field — Specifies the size of the operation:
    00 — byte operation.
    01 — word operation.
    10 — long operation.
Effective Address field — Specifies the destination operand. Only data alterable addressing modes are allowed as shown:

Addressing Mode	Mode	Register	Addressing Mode	Mode	Register
Dn	000	register number	d(An, Xi)	110	register number
An	—	—	Abs.W	111	000
(An)	010	register number	Abs.L	111	001
(An)+	011	register number	d(PC)	—	—
–(An)	100	register number	d(PC, Xi)	—	—
d(An)	101	register number	Imm	—	—

Immediate field — (Data immediately following the instruction):
    If size = 00, then the data is the low order byte of the immediate word.
    If size = 01, then the data is the entire immediate word.
    If size = 10, then the data is the next two immediate words.

CMPM   Compare Memory   CMPM

Operation: (Destination) − (Source)

**Assembler
Syntax:**   CMPM (Ay) + , (Ax) +

Attributes: Size = (Byte, Word, Long)

Description: Subtract the source operand from the destination operand, and set the condition codes according to the results; the destination location is not changed. The operands are always addressed with the postincrement addressing mode using the address registers specified in the instruction. The size of the operation may be specified to be byte, word, or long.

Condition Codes:

X	N	Z	V	C
—	*	*	*	*

N   Set if the result is negative. Cleared otherwise.
Z   Set if the result is zero. Cleared otherwise.
V   Set if an overflow is generated. Cleared otherwise.
C   Set if a borrow is generated. Cleared otherwise.
X   Not affected.

Instruction Format:

15	14	13	12	11	10	9	8	7	6	5	4	3	2	1	0
1	0	1	1	Register Rx			1	Size		0	0	1	Register Ry		

Instruction Fields:

Register Rx field — (always the destination) Specifies an address register for the postincrement addressing mode.
Size field — Specifies the size of the operation:
    00 — byte operation.
    01 — word operation.
    10 — long operation.
Register Ry field — (always the source) Specifies an address register for the postincrement addressing mode.

DBcc

Test Condition, Decrement, and Branch

DBcc

Operation: If (condition false)
    then Dn − 1 → Dn;
    If Dn ≠ − 1
        then PC + d → PC
    else PC + 2 → PC (Fall through to next instruction)

Assembler Syntax: DBcc Dn, <label>

Attributes: Size = (Word)

Description: This instruction is a looping primitive of three parameters: a condition, a data register, and a displacement. The instruction first tests the condition to determine if the termination condition for the loop has been met, and if so, no operation is performed. If the termination condition is not true, the low order 16 bits of the counter data register are decremented by one. If the result is − 1, the counter is exhausted and execution continues with the next instruction. If the result is not equal to − 1, execution continues at the location indicated by the current value of PC plus the sign-extended 16-bit displacement. The value in PC is the current instruction location plus two "cc" may specify the following conditions:

CC	carry clear	0100	$\overline{C}$	LS	low or same	0011	$C+Z$
CS	carry set	0101	C	LT	less than	1101	$N \cdot \overline{V} + \overline{N} \cdot V$
EQ	equal	0111	Z	MI	minus	1011	N
F	false	0001	0	NE	not equal	0110	$\overline{Z}$
GE	greater or equal	1100	$N \cdot V + \overline{N} \cdot \overline{V}$	PL	plus	1010	$\overline{N}$
GT	greater than	1110	$N \cdot V \cdot \overline{Z} + \overline{N} \cdot \overline{V} \cdot \overline{Z}$	T	true	0000	1
HI	high	0010	$\overline{C} \cdot \overline{Z}$	VC	overflow clear	1000	$\overline{V}$
LE	less or equal	1111	$Z + N \cdot \overline{V} + \overline{N} \cdot V$	VS	overflow set	1001	V

Condition Codes: Not affected.

Instruction Format:

15	14	13	12	11	10	9	8	7	6	5	4	3	2	1	0
0	1	0	1	Condition				1	1	0	0	1	Register		
Displacement															

Instruction Fields:

Condition field — One of the sixteen conditions discussed in description.
Register field — Specifies the data register which is the counter.
Displacement field — Specifies the distance of the branch (in bytes).

Notes:

1. The terminating condition is like that defined by the UNTIL loop constructs of high-level languages. For example: DBMI can be stated as "decrement and branch until minus."

— Continued —

Notes: (Continued)

2. Most assemblers accept DBRA for DBF for use when no condition is required for termination of a loop.

3. There are two basic ways of entering a loop; at the beginning or by branching to the trailing DBcc instruction. If a loop structure terminated with DBcc is entered at the beginning, the control index count must be one less than the number of loop executions desired. This count is useful for indexed addressing modes and dynamically specified bit operations. However, when entering a loop by branching directly to the trailing DBcc instruction, the control index should equal the loop execution count. In this case, if a zero count occurs, the DBcc instruction will not branch causing complete bypass of the main loop.

DIVS

Signed Divide

DIVS

Operation: (Destination)/(Source) → Destination

**Assembler
Syntax:** DIVS < ea >, Dn

Attributes: Size = (Word)

Description: Divide the destination operand by the source operand and store the result in the destination. The destination operand is a long operand (32 bits) and the source operand is a word operand (16 bits). The operation is performed using signed arithmetic. The result is a 32-bit result such that:
1. The quotient is in the lower word (least significant 16-bits).
2. The remainder is in the upper word (most significant 16-bits).

The sign of the remainder is always the same as the dividend unless the remainder is equal to zero. Two special conditions may arise:
1. Division by zero causes a trap.
2. Overflow may be detected and set before completion of the instruction. If overflow is detected, the condition is flagged but the operands are unaffected.

Condition Codes:

X	N	Z	V	C
—	*	*	*	0

N Set if the quotient is negative. Cleared otherwise. Undefined if overflow.

Z Set if the quotient is zero. Cleared otherwise. Undefined if overflow.

V Set if division overflow is detected. Cleared otherwise.

C Always cleared.

X Not affected.

Instruction Format:

15	14	13	12	11	10	9	8	7	6	5	4	3	2	1	0
1	0	0	0	Register			1	1	1	Effective Address Mode			Register		

Instruction Fields:

Register field — Specifies any of the eight data registers. This field always specifies the destination operand.

Effective Address field — Specifies the source operand. Only data addressing modes are allowed as shown:

Addressing Mode	Mode	Register	Addressing Mode	Mode	Register
Dn	000	register number	d(An, Xi)	110	register number
An	—	—	Abs.W	111	000
(An)	010	register number	Abs.L	111	001
(An) +	011	register number	d(PC)	111	010
− (An)	100	register number	d(PC, Xi)	111	011
d(An)	101	register number	Imm	111	100

Note: Overflow occurs if the quotient is larger than a 16-bit signed integer.

DIVU

Unsigned Divide

Operation: (Destination)/(Source) → Destination

**Assembler
Syntax:** DIVU <ea>, Dn

Attributes: Size = (Word)

Description: Divide the destination operand by the source operand and store the result in the destination. The destination operand is a long operand (32 bits) and the source operand is a word (16 bit) operand. The operation is performed using unsigned arithmetic. The result is a 32-bit result such that:
　　1. The quotient is in the lower word (least significnat 16 bits).
　　2. The remainder is in the upper word (most significant 16 bits).
Two special conditions may arise:
　　1. Division by zero causes a trap.
　　2. Overflow may be detected and set before completion of the instruction. If overflow is detected, the condition is flagged but the operands are unaffected.

Condition Codes:

X	N	Z	V	C
—	*	*	*	0

N　Set if the most significant bit of the quotient is set. Cleared otherwise. Undefined if overflow.
Z　Set if the quotient is zero. Cleared otherwise. Undefined if overflow.
V　Set if division overflow is detected. Cleared otherwise.
C　Always cleared.
X　Not affected.

Instruction Format:

15	14	13	12	11 10 9	8	7	6	5 4 3	2 1 0
1	0	0	0	Register	0	1	1	Effective Address Mode	Register

Instruction Fields:

Register field — specifies any of the eight data registers. This field always specifies the destination operand.

Effective Address field — Specifies the source operand. Only data addressing modes are allowed as shown:

Addressing Mode	Mode	Register	Addressing Mode	Mode	Register
Dn	000	register number	d(An, Xi)	110	register number
An	—	—	Abs.W	111	000
(An)	010	register number	Abs.L	111	001
(An) +	011	register number	d(PC)	111	010
– (An)	100	register number	d(PC, Xi)	111	011
d(An)	101	register number	Imm	111	100

Note: Overflow occurs if the quotient is larger than a 16-bit unsigned integer.

EOR

Exclusive OR Logical

Operation: (Source) ⊕ (Destination) → Destination

**Assembler
Syntax:** EOR Dn, <ea>

Attributes: Size = (Byte, Word, Long)

Description: Exclusive OR the source operand to the destination operand and store the result in the destination location. The size of the operation may be specified to be byte, word, or long. This operation is restricted to data registers as the source operand. The destination operand is specified in the effective address field.

Condition Codes:

X	N	Z	V	C
—	*	*	0	0

N Set if the most significant bit of the result is set. Cleared otherwise.
Z Set if the result is zero. Cleared otherwise.
V Always cleared.
C Always cleared.
X Not affected.

Instruction Format:

15	14	13	12	11	10	9	8	7	6	5	4	3	2	1	0
1	0	1	1	Register			Op-Mode			Effective Address Mode | Register					

Instruction Fields:

Register field — Specifies any of the eight data registers.
Op-Mode field —

Byte	Word	Long	Operation
100	101	110	(<ea>) ⊕ (<Dx>) → <ea>

Effective Address field — Specifies the destination operand. Only data alterable addressing modes are allowed as shown:

Addressing Mode	Mode	Register	Addressing Mode	Mode	Register
Dn	000	register number	d(An, Xi)	110	register number
An	—	—	Abs.W	111	000
(An)	010	register number	Abs.L	111	001
(An)+	011	register number	d(PC)	—	—
−(An)	100	register number	d(PC, Xi)	—	—
d(An)	101	register number	Imm	—	—

Note: Memory to data register operations are not allowed. EORI is used when the source is immediate data. Most assemblers automatically make this distinction.

EORI
Exclusive OR Immediate
EORI

Operation: Immediate Data ⊕ (Destination) → Destination

**Assembler
Syntax:** EORI #<data>, <ea>

Attributes: Size = (Byte, Word, Long)

Description: Exclusive OR the immediate data to the destination operand and store the result in the destination location. The size of the operation may be specified to be byte, word, or long. The immediate data matches the operation size.

Condition Codes:

X	N	Z	V	C
—	*	*	0	0

N Set if the most significant bit of the result is set. Cleared otherwise.
Z Set if the result is zero. Cleared otherwise.
V Always cleared.
C Always cleared.
X Not affected.

Instruction Format:

15	14	13	12	11	10	9	8	7	6	5 4 3	2 1 0
0	0	0	0	1	0	1	0	Size		Effective Address Mode | Register	
Word Data (16 bits)								Byte Data (8 bits)			
Long Data (32 bits, including previous word)											

Instruction Fields:

Size field — Specifies the size of the operation:
00 — byte operation.
01 — word operation.
10 — long operation.

Effective Address field — Specifies the destination operand. Only data alterable addressing modes are allowed as shown:

Addressing Mode	Mode	Register	Addressing Mode	Mode	Register
Dn	000	register number	d(An, Xi)	110	register number
An	—	—	Abs.W	111	000
(An)	010	register number	Abs.L	111	001
(An)+	011	register number	d(PC)	—	—
−(An)	100	register number	d(PC, Xi)	—	—
d(An)	101	register number	Imm	—	—

Immediate field — (Data immediately following the instruction):
If size = 00, then the data is the low order byte of the immediate word.
If size = 01, then the data is the entire immediate word.
If size = 10, then the data is the next two immediate words.

EORI
to CCR

Exclusive OR Immediate to Condition Codes

EORI
to CCR

Operation: (Source) ⊕ CCR → CCR

Assembler
Syntax: EORI #xxx, CCR

Attributes: Size = (Byte)

Description: Exclusive OR the immediate operand with the condition codes and store the result in the low-order byte of the status register.

Condition Codes:

X	N	Z	V	C
*	*	*	*	*

N   Changed if bit 3 of immediate operand is one. Unchanged otherwise.
Z   Changed if bit 2 of immediate operand is one. Unchanged otherwise.
V   Changed if bit 1 of immediate operand is one. Unchanged otherwise.
C   Changed if bit 0 of immediate operand is one. Unchanged otherwise.
X   Changed if bit 4 of immediate operand is one. Unchanged otherwise.

Instruction Format:

15	14	13	12	11	10	9	8	7	6	5	4	3	2	1	0
0	0	0	0	1	0	1	0	0	0	1	1	1	1	0	0
0	0	0	0	0	0	0	0	Byte Data (8 bits)							

EORI
to SR

EORI
to SR

Operation:　If supervisor state
　　　　　　　then (Source) $\oplus$ SR $\rightarrow$ SR
　　　　　　　else TRAP

Assembler
Syntax:　　EORI #xxx, SR

Attributes:　Size = (Word)

Description: Exclusive OR the immediate operand with the contents of the status register and store the result in the status register. All bits of the status register are affected.

Condition Codes:

X	N	Z	V	C
*	*	*	*	*

N　Changed if bit 3 of immediate operand is one. Unchanged otherwise.
Z　Changed if bit 2 of immediate operand is one. Unchanged otherwise.
V　Changed if bit 1 of immediate operand is one. Unchanged otherwise.
C　Changed if bit 0 of immediate operand is one. Unchanged otherwise.
X　Changed if bit 4 of immediate operand is one. Unchanged otherwise.

Instruction Format:

15	14	13	12	11	10	9	8	7	6	5	4	3	2	1	0
0	0	0	0	1	0	1	0	0	1	1	1	1	1	0	0
Word Data (16 bits)																

96

EXG

Operation: Rx ↔ Ry

**Assembler
Syntax:**   EXG Rx, Ry

Attributes: Size = (Long)

Description: Exchange the contents of two registers. This exchange is always a long (32 bit) operation. Exchange works in three modes:
     1. Exchange data registers.
     2. Exchange address registers.
     3. Exchange a data register and an address register.

Condition Codes: Not affected.

Instruction Format:

15	14	13	12	11 10 9	8	7 6 5 4 3	2 1 0
1	1	0	0	Register Rx	1	Op-Mode	Register Ry

Instruction Fields:

Register Rx field — Specifies either a data register or an address register depending on the mode. If the exchange is between data and address registers, this field always specifies the data register.

Op-Mode field — Specifies whether exchanging:
     01000 — data registers.
     01001 — address registers.
     10001 — data register and address register.

Register Ry field — Specifies either a data register or an address register depending on the mode. If the exchange is between data and address registers, this field always specifies the address register.

EXT

Sign Extend

Operation: (Destination) Sign-extended → Destination

**Assembler
Syntax:**   EXT Dn

Attributes: Size = (Word, Long)

Description: Extend the sign bit of a data register from a byte to a word or from a word to
a long operand depending on the size selected. If the operation is word
sized, bit [7] of the designated data register is copied to bits [15:8] of that
data register. If the operation is long sized, bit [15] of the designated data
register is copied to bits [31:16] of that data register.

Condition Codes:

X	N	Z	V	C
—	*	*	0	0

N   Set if the result is negative. Cleared otherwise.
Z   Set if the result is zero. Cleared otherwise.
V   Always cleared.
C   Always cleared.
X   Not affected.

Instruction Format:

15	14	13	12	11	10	9	8	7	6	5	4	3	2	1	0
0	1	0	0	1	0	0	Op-Mode			0	0	0	Register		

Instruction Fields:

Op-Mode Field — Specifies the size of the sign-extension operation:
010 — Sign-extend low order byte of data register to word.
011 — Sign-extend low order word of data register to long.
Register field — Specifies the data register whose content is to be sign-extended.

ILLEGAL   Illegal Instruction   ILLEGAL

Operation: PC→ −(SSP); SR→ −(SSP)
(Illegal Instruction Vector)→ PC

Attributes: None

Description: This bit pattern causes an illegal instruction exception. All other illegal instruction bit patterns are reserved for future extension of the instruction set.

Condition Codes: Not affected.

Instruction Format:

15	14	13	12	11	10	9	8	7	6	5	4	3	2	1	0
0	1	0	0	1	0	1	0	1	1	1	1	1	1	0	0

JMP

Jump

Operation: Destination → PC

**Assembler
Syntax:** JMP <ea>

Attributes: Unsized

Description: Program execution continues at the effective address specified by the instruction. The address is specified by the control addressing modes.

Condition Codes: Not affected.

Instruction Format:

15	14	13	12	11	10	9	8	7	6	5 4 3	2 1 0
0	1	0	0	1	1	1	0	1	1	Effective Address Mode	Register

Instruction Fields:

Effective Address field — Specifies the address of the next instruction. Only control addressing modes are allowed as shown:

Addressing Mode	Mode	Register	Addressing Mode	Mode	Register
Dn	—	—	d(An, Xi)	110	register number
An	—	—	Abs.W	111	000
(An)	010	register number	Abs.L	111	001
(An)+	—	—	d(PC)	111	010
−(An)	—	—	d(PC, Xi)	111	011
d(An)	101	register number	Imm	—	—

100

JSR

Jump to Subroutine

JSR

Operation: PC → − (SP); Destination → PC

**Assembler
Syntax:** JSR <ea>

Attributes: Unsized

Description: The long word address of the instruction immediately following the JSR instruction is pushed onto the system stack. Program execution then continues at the address specifed in the instruction.

Condition Codes: Not affected.

Instruction Format:

15	14	13	12	11	10	9	8	7	6	5	4	3	2	1	0
0	1	0	0	1	1	1	0	1	0	\multicolumn{6}{c}{Effective Address Mode ∣ Register}

Instruction Fields:

Effective Address field — Specifies the address of the next instruction.
Only control addressing modes are allowed as shown:

Addressing Mode	Mode	Register	Addressing Mode	Mode	Register
Dn	—	—	d(An, Xi)	110	register number
An	—	—	Abs.W	111	000
(An)	010	register number	Abs.L	111	001
(An) +	—	—	d(PC)	111	010
− (An)	—	—	d(PC, Xi)	111	011
d(An)	101	register number	Imm	—	—

LEA

Load Effective Address

Operation: Destination → An

**Assembler
Syntax:** LEA <ea>, An

Attributes: Size = (Long)

Description: The effective address is loaded into the specified address register. All 32 bits of the address register are affected by this instruction.

Condition Codes: Not affected.

Instruction Format:

15	14	13	12	11 10 9	8	7	6	5 4 3	2 1 0
0	1	0	0	Register	1	1	1	Effective Address Mode	Register

Instruction Fields:

Register field — Specifies the address register which is to be loaded with the effective address.

Effective Address field — Specifies the address to be loaded into the address register. Only control addressing modes are allowed as shown:

Addressing Mode	Mode	Register	Addressing Mode	Mode	Register
Dn	—	—	d(An, Xi)	110	register number
An	—	—	Abs.W	111	000
(An)	010	register number	Abs.L	111	001
(An) +	—	—	d(PC)	111	010
– (An)	—	—	d(PC, Xi)	111	011
d(An)	101	register number	Imm	—	—

102

LINK

Link and Allocate

LINK

Operation: An → −(SP); SP → An; SP + d → SP

**Assembler
Syntax:**   LINK An, #<displacement>

Attributes: Unsized

Description: The current content of the specified address register is pushed onto the stack. After the push, the address register is loaded from the updated stack pointer. Finally, the 16-bit sign-extended displacement is added to the stack pointer. The content of the address register occupies two words on the stack. A negative displacement is specified to allocate stack area.

Condition Codes: Not affected.

Instruction Format:

15	14	13	12	11	10	9	8	7	6	5	4	3	2	1	0
0	1	0	0	1	1	1	0	0	1	0	1	0	Register		
Displacement															

Instruction Fields:

Register field — Specifies the address register through which the link is to be constructed.

Displacement field — Specifies the twos complement integer which is to be added to the stack pointer.

Note: LINK and UNLK can be used to maintain a linked list of local data and parameter areas on the stack for nested subroutine calls.

LSL, LSR   Logical Shift   LSL, LSR

Operation: (Destination) Shifted by <count> → Destination

Assembler   LSd Dx, Dy
Syntax: LSd #<data>, Dy
           LSd <ea>

Attributes: Size = (Byte, Word, Long)

Description: Shift the bits of the operand in the direction specified. The carry bit receives the last bit shifted out of the operand. The shift count for the shifting of a register may be specified in two different ways:

1. Immediate — the shift count is specified in the instruction (shift range 1-8).
2. Register — the shift count is contained in a data register specified in the instruction.

The size of the operation may be specified to be byte, word, or long. The content of memory may be shifted one bit only and the operand size is restricted to a word.

For LSL, the operand is shifted left; the number of positions shifted is the shift count. Bits shifted out of the high order bit go to both the carry and the extend bits; zeroes are shifted into the low order bit.

LSL:

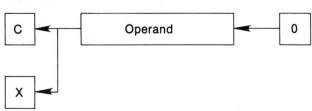

For LSR, the operand is shifted right; the number of positions shifted is the shift count. Bits shifted out of the low order bit go to both the carry and the extend bits; zeroes are shifted into the high order bit.

LSR:

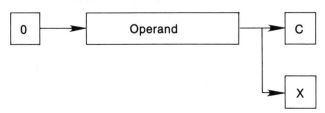

— Continued —

LSL, LSR   Logical Shift   LSL, LSR

Condition Codes:

X	N	Z	V	C
*	*	*	0	*

N   Set if the result is negative. Cleared otherwise.
Z   Set if the result is zero. Cleared otherwise.
V   Always cleared.
C   Set according to the last bit shifted out of the operand. Cleared for a shift count of zero.
X   Set according to the last bit shifted out of the operand. Unaffected for a shift count of zero.

Instruction Format (Register Shifts):

15	14	13	12	11 10 9	8	7 6	5	4	3	2 1 0
1	1	1	0	Count/Register	dr	Size	i/r	0	1	Register

Instruction Fields (Register Shifts):

Count/Register field —

If i/r = 0, the shift count is specified in this field. The values 0, 1-7 represent a range of 8, 1 to 7 respectively.

If i/r = 1, the shift count (modulo 64) is contained in the data register specified in this field.

dr field — Specifies the direction of the shift:

0 — shift right.

1 — shift left.

Size field — Specifies the size of the operation:

00 — byte operation.

01 — word operation.

10 — long operation.

i/r field —

If i/r = 0, specifies immediate shift count.

If i/r = 1, specifies register shift count.

Register field — Specifies a data register whose content is to be shifted.

— Continued —

LSL, LSR   Logical Shift   LSL,LSR

Instruction Format (Memory Shifts):

15	14	13	12	11	10	9	8	7	6	5 4 3	2 1 0
1	1	1	0	0	0	1	dr	1	1	Effective Address Mode	Register

Instruction Fields (Memory Shifts):

dr field — Specifies the direction of the shift:

0 — shift right.

1 — shift left.

Effective Address field — Specifies the operand to be shifted. Only memory alterable addressing modes are allowed as shown:

Addressing Mode	Mode	Register	Addressing Mode	Mode	Register
Dn	—	—	d(An, Xi)	110	register number
An	—	—	Abs.W	111	000
(An)	010	register number	Abs.L	111	001
(An)+	011	register number	d(PC)	—	—
−(An)	100	register number	d(PC, Xi)	—	—
d(An)	101	register number	Imm	—	—

106

MOVE  MOVE

Move Data from Source to Destination

Operation: (Source) → Destination

**Assembler
Syntax:**   MOVE <ea>, <ea>

Attributes: Size = (Byte, Word, Long)

Description: Move the content of the source to the destination location. The data is examined as it is moved, and the condition codes set accordingly. The size of the operation may be specified to be byte, word, or long.

Condition Codes:

X	N	Z	V	C
—	*	*	0	0

N   Set if the result is negative. Cleared otherwise.
Z   Set if the result is zero. Cleared otherwise.
V   Always cleared.
C   Always cleared.
X   Not affected.

Instruction Format:

15	14	13 12	11 10 9	8 7 6	5 4 3	2 1 0
0	0	Size	Destination Register	Mode	Source Mode	Register

Instruction Fields:

Size field — Specifies the size of the operand to be moved:
  01 — byte operation.
  11 — word operation.
  10 — long operation.
Destination Effective Address field — Specifies the destination location. Only data alterable addressing modes are allowed as shown:

Addressing Mode	Mode	Register	Addressing Mode	Mode	Register
Dn	000	register number	d(An, Xi)	110	register number
An	—	—	Abs.W	111	000
(An)	010	register number	Abs.L	111	001
(An) +	011	register number	d(PC)	—	—
– (An)	100	register number	d(PC, Xi)	—	—
d(An)	101	register number	Imm	—	—

— Continued —

MOVE

Move Data from Source to Destination **MOVE**

Instruction Fields: (Continued)

Source Effective Address field — Specifies the source operand. All addressing modes are allowed as shown:

Addressing Mode	Mode	Register	Addressing Mode	Mode	Register
Dn	000	register number	d(An, Xi)	110	register number
An*	001	register number	Abs.W	111	000
(An)	010	register number	Abs.L	111	001
(An) +	011	register number	d(PC)	111	010
− (An)	100	register number	d(PC, Xi)	111	011
d(An)	101	register number	Imm	111	100

*For byte size operation, address register direct is not allowed.

Notes:
1. MOVEA is used when the destination is an address register. Most assemblers automatically make this distinction.
2. MOVEQ can also be used for certain operations on data registers.

MOVE
from CCR

MOVE
from CCR

Operation: CCR→Destination

**Assembler
Syntax:** MOVE CCR, <ea>

Attributes: Size = (Word)

Description: The content of the status register is moved to the destination location. The source operand is a word, but only the low order byte contains the condition codes. The upper byte is all zeros.

Condition Codes: Not affected.

Instruction Format:

15	14	13	12	11	10	9	8	7	6	5	4	3	2	1	0
0	1	0	0	0	0	1	0	1	1	Effective Address Mode			Register		

Instruction Fields:

Effective Address field — Specifies the destination location.
Only data alterable addressing modes are allowed as shown:

Addressing Mode	Mode	Register
Dn	000	register number
An	—	—
(An)	010	register number
(An)+	011	register number
−(An)	100	register number
d(An)	101	register number

Addressing Mode	Mode	Register
d(An, Xi)	110	register number
Abs.W	111	000
Abs.L	111	001
d(PC)	—	—
d(PC, Xi)	—	—
Imm	—	—

Note: MOVE to CCR is a word operation. AND, OR, and EOR to CCR are byte operations.

MC68010

MOVE to CCR

MOVE to CCR

Operation: (Source) → CCR

Assembler Syntax: MOVE <ea>, CCR

Attributes: Size = (Word)

Description: The content of the source operand is moved to the condition codes. The source operand is a word, but only the low order byte is used to update the condition codes. The upper byte is ignored.

Condition Codes:

X	N	Z	V	C
*	*	*	*	*

N   Set the same as bit 3 of the source operand.
Z   Set the same as bit 2 of the source operand.
V   Set the same as bit 1 of the source operand.
C   Set the same as bit 0 of the source operand.
X   Set the same as bit 4 of the source operand.

Instruction Format:

15	14	13	12	11	10	9	8	7	6	5 4 3	2 1 0
0	1	0	0	0	1	0	0	1	1	Effective Address Mode	Register

Instruction Fields:

Effective Address field — Specifies the location of the source operand. Only data addressing modes are allowed as shown:

Addressing Mode	Mode	Register	Addressing Mode	Mode	Register
Dn	000	register number	d(An, Xi)	110	register number
An	—	—	Abs.W	111	000
(An)	010	register number	Abs.L	111	001
(An)+	011	register number	d(PC)	111	010
−(An)	100	register number	d(PC, Xi)	111	011
d(An)	101	register number	Imm	111	100

Note: MOVE to CCR is a word operation. AND, OR, and EOR to CCR are byte operations.

MOVE
to SR

MOVE
to SR

Operation: If supervisor state
                     then (Source)→ SR
                     else TRAP

Assembler
Syntax: MOVE <ea>, SR

Attributes: Size = (Word)

Description: The content of the source operand is moved to the status register. The source operand is a word and all bits of the status register are affected.

Condition Codes: Set according to the source operand.

Instruction Format:

15	14	13	12	11	10	9	8	7	6	5 4 3 2 1 0
0	1	0	0	0	1	1	0	1	1	Effective Address Mode | Register

Instruction Fields:

Effective Address field — Specifies the location of the source operand. Only data addressing modes are allowed as shown:

Addressing Mode	Mode	Register	Addressing Mode	Mode	Register
Dn	000	register number	d(An, Xi)	110	register number
An	—	—	Abs.W	111	000
(An)	010	register number	Abs.L	111	001
(An) +	011	register number	d(PC)	111	010
− (An)	100	register number	d(PC, Xi)	111	011
d(An)	101	register number	Imm	111	100

111

MOVE from SR

MOVE from SR

Operation: SR → Destination

**Assembler
Syntax:** MOVE SR, <ea>

Attributes: Size = (Word)

Description: The content of the status register is moved to the destination location. The operand size is a word.

Condition Codes: Not affected.

Instruction Format:

15	14	13	12	11	10	9	8	7	6	5 4 3	2 1 0
0	1	0	0	0	0	0	0	1	1	Effective Address Mode	Register

Instruction Fields:

Effective Address field — Specifies the destination location. Only data alterable addressing modes are allowed as shown:

Addressing Mode	Mode	Register	Addressing Mode	Mode	Register
Dn	000	register number	d(An, Xi)	110	register number
An	—	—	Abs.W	111	000
(An)	010	register number	Abs.L	111	001
(An) +	011	register number	d(PC)	—	—
– (An)	100	register number	d(PC, Xi)	—	—
d(An)	101	register number	Imm	—	—

Note: A memory destination is read before it is written to.

MOVE from SR

MOVE from SR

**Move from the Status Register
(Privileged Instruction)**

Operation: If supervisor state
                         then SR→Destination
                         else TRAP

**Assembler
Syntax:**   MOVE SR, <ea>

Attributes: Size = (Word)

Description: The content of the status register is moved to the destination location. The operand size is a word.

Condition Codes: Not affected.

Instruction Format:

15	14	13	12	11	10	9	8	7	6	5	4	3	2	1	0
0	1	0	0	0	0	0	0	1	1	Effective Address Mode			Register		

Instruction Fields:

   Effective Address field — Specifies the destination location. Only data alterable addressing modes are allowed as shown:

Addressing Mode	Mode	Register	Addressing Mode	Mode	Register
Dn	000	register number	d(An, Xi)	110	register number
An	—	—	Abs.W	111	000
(An)	010	register number	Abs.L	111	001
(An)+	011	register number	d(PC)	—	—
−(An)	100	register number	d(PC, Xi)	—	—
d(An)	101	register number	Imm	—	—

NOTE: Use the MOVE from CCR instruction to access the conditon codes.

MC68010

113

Move User Stack Pointer
(Privileged Instruction)

Operation: If supervisor state
then USP→ An;
An→ USP
else TRAP

Assembler MOVE USP, An
Syntax: MOVE An, USP

Attributes: Size = (Long)

Description: The contents of the user stack pointer are transferred to or from the specified address register.

Condition Codes: Not affected.

Instruction Format:

15	14	13	12	11	10	9	8	7	6	5	4	3	2	1	0
0	1	0	0	1	1	1	0	0	1	1	0	dr	Register		

Instruction Fields:
dr field — Specifies the direction of transfer:
0 — transfer the address register to the USP.
1 — transfer the USP to the address register.
Register field — Specifies the address register to or from which the user stack pointer is to be transferred.

MOVEA   Move Address   MOVEA

Operation: (Source) → Destination

**Assembler
Syntax:**   MOVEA <ea>, An

Attributes: Size = (Word, Long)

Description: Move the content of the source to the destination address register. The size of the operation may be specified to be word or long. Word size source operands are sign extended to 32 bit quantities before the operation is done.

Condition Codes: Not affected.

Instruction Format:

15	14	13	12	11	10	9	8	7	6	5	4	3	2	1	0
0	0	Size		Destination Register			0	0	1	Source Mode			Register		

Instruction Fields:

Size field — Specifies the size of the operand to be moved:
11 — Word operation. The source operand is sign-extended to a long operand and all 32 bits are loaded into the address register.
10 — Long operation.
Destination Register field — Specifies the destination address register.
Source Effective Address field — Specifies the location of the source operand. All addressing modes are allowed as shown:

Addressing Mode	Mode	Register	Addressing Mode	Mode	Register
Dn	000	register number	d(An, Xi)	110	register number
An	001	register number	Abs.W	111	000
(An)	010	register number	Abs.L	111	001
(An) +	011	register number	d(PC)	111	010
– (An)	100	register number	d(PC, Xi)	111	011
d(An)	101	register number	Imm	111	100

MOVEC

Move to/from Control Register
(Privileged Instruction)

MOVEC

Operation: If supervisor state
then Rc → Rn, Rn → Rc
else TRAP

Assembler MOVEC Rc, Rn
Syntax: MOVEC Rn, Rc

Attributes: Size = (Long)

Description: Copy the contents of the specified control register to the specified general register or copy the contents of the specified general register to the specified control register. This is always a 32-bit transfer even though the control register may be implemented with fewer bits. Unimplemented bits are read as zeros.

Condition Codes: Not affected.

Instruction Format:

15	14	13	12	11	10	9	8	7	6	5	4	3	2	1	0
0	1	0	0	1	1	1	0	0	1	1	1	1	0	1	dr
A/D	Register			Control Register											

Instruction Fields:

dr field — Specifies the direction of the transfer:
   0—control register to general register.
   1—general register to control register.
A/D field — Specifies the type of general register:
   0—data register.
   1—address register.
Register field — Specifies the register number.
Control Register field — Specifies the control register.
Currently defined control registers are:

Binary	Hex	Name/Function
0000 0000 0000	000	Source Function Code (SFC) register.
0000 0000 0001	001	Destination Function Code (DFC) register.
1000 0000 0000	800	User Stack Pointer.
1000 0000 0001	801	Vector Base Register for exception vector table.

All other codes cause an illegal instruction exception.

MC68010

116

MOVEM   Move Multiple Registers   MOVEM

Operation: Registers → Destination
(Source) → Registers

Assembler   MOVEM < register list >, < ea >
Syntax: MOVEM < ea >, < register list >

Attributes: Size = (Word, Long)

Description: Selected registers are transferred to or from consecutive memory location starting at the location specified by the effective address. A register is transferred if the bit corresponding to that register is set in the mask field. The instruction selects how much of each register is transferred; either the entire long word can be moved or just the low order word. In the case of a word transfer to the registers, each word is sign-extended to 32 bits (also data registers) and the resulting long word loaded into the associated register.

MOVEM allows three forms of address modes: the control modes, the predecrement mode, or the postincrement mode. If the effective address is in one of the control modes, the registers are transferred starting at the specified address and up through higher addresses. The order of transfer is from data register 0 to data register 7, then from address register 0 to address register 7.

If the effective address is in the predecrement mode, only a register to memory operation is allowed. The registers are stored starting at the specified address minus two and down through lower addresses. The order of storing is from address register 7 to address register 0, then from data register 7 to data register 0. The decremented address register is updated to contain the address of the last word stored.

If the effective address is in the postincrement mode, only a memory to register operation is allowed. The registers are loaded starting at the specified address and up through higher addresses. The order of loading is the same as for the control mode addressing. The incremented address register is updated to contain the address of the last word loaded plus two.

Condition Codes: Not affected.

Instruction Format:

15	14	13	12	11	10	9	8	7	6	5	4	3	2	1	0
0	1	0	0	1	dr	0	0	1	Sz	Effective Address Mode			Register		
Register List Mask															

— Continued —

MOVEM   Move Multiple Registers   MOVEM

Instruction Fields:

dr field:

Specifies the direction of the transfer:

0 — register to memory

1 — memory to register.

Sz field — Specifies the size of the registers being transferred:

0 — word transfer.

1 — long transfer.

Effective Address field — Specifies the memory address to or from which the registers are to be moved.

For register to memory transfer, only control alterable addressing modes or the predecrement addressing mode are allowed as shown:

Addressing Mode	Mode	Register	Addressing Mode	Mode	Register
Dn	—	—	d(An, Xi)	110	register number
An	—	—	Abs.W	111	000
(An)	010	register number	Abs.L	111	001
(An)+	—	—	d(PC)	—	—
−(An)	100	register number	d(PC, Xi)	—	—
d(An)	101	register number	Imm	—	—

For memory to register transfer, only control addressing modes or the postincrement addressing mode are allowed as shown:

Addressing Mode	Mode	Register	Addressing Mode	Mode	Register
Dn	—	—	d(An, Xi)	110	register number
An	—	—	Abs.W	111	000
(An)	010	register number	Abs.L	111	001
(An)+	011	register number	d(PC)	111	010
−(An)	—	—	d(PC, Xi)	111	011
d(An)	101	register number	Imm	—	—

Register List Mask field — Specifies which registers are to be transferred. The low order bit corresponds to the first register to be transferred; the high bit corresponds to the last register to be transferred. Thus, both for control modes and for the postincrement mode addresses, the mask correspondence is

15	14	13	12	11	10	9	8	7	6	5	4	3	2	1	0
A7	A6	A5	A4	A3	A2	A1	A0	D7	D6	D5	D4	D3	D2	D1	D0

while for the predecrement mode addresses, the mask correspondence is

15	14	13	12	11	10	9	8	7	6	5	4	3	2	1	0
D0	D1	D2	D3	D4	D5	D6	D7	A0	A1	A2	A3	A4	A5	A6	A7

Note: An extra read bus cycle occurs for memory operands. This amounts to a memory word at one address higher than expected being addressed during operation.

MOVEP   Move Peripheral Data   MOVEP

Operation: (Source)→ Destination

Assembler   MOVEP Dx, d(Ay)
Syntax: MOVEP d(Ay), Dx

Attributes: Size = (Word, Long)

Description: Data is transferred between a data register and alternate bytes of memory, starting at the location specified and incrementing by two. The high order byte of the data register is transferred first and the low order byte is transferred last. The memory address is specified using the address register indirect plus displacement addressing mode. If the address is even, all the transfers are made on the high order half of the data bus; if the address is odd, all the transfers are made on the low order half of the data bus.

Example: Long transfer to/from an even address.

Byte organization in register

31	24	23	16	15	8	7	0
hi-order		mid-upper		mid-lower		low-order	

Byte organization in memory (low address at top)

15	14	13	12	11	10	9	8	7	6	5	4	3	2	1	0
hi-order															
mid-upper															
mid-lower															
low-order															

Example: Word transfer to/from an odd address.

Byte organization in register

31	24	23	16	15	8	7	0
				hi-order		low-order	

Byte organization in memory (low address at top)

15	14	13	12	11	10	9	8	7	6	5	4	3	2	1	0
								hi-order							
								low-order							

Condition Codes: Not affected.

— Continued —

MOVEP Move Peripheral Data MOVEP

Instruction Format:

15	14	13	12	11 10 9	8 7 6	5	4	3	2 1 0
0	0	0	0	Data Register	Op-Mode	0	0	1	Address Register
				Displacement					

Instruction Fields:

Data Register field — Specifies the data register to or from which the data is to be transferred.

Op-Mode field — Specifies the direction and size of the operation:
  100 — transfer word from memory to register.
  101 — transfer long from memory to register.
  110 — transfer word from register to memory.
  111 — transfer long from register to memory.

Address Register field — Specifies the address register which is used in the address register indirect plus displacement addressing mode.

Displacement field — Specifies the displacement which is used in calculating the operand address.

MOVEQ　　　Move Quick　　　MOVEQ

Operation:　Immediate Data → Destination

**Assembler
Syntax:**　MOVEQ #<data>, Dn

Attributes:　Size = (Long)

Description:　Move immediate data to a data register. The data is contained in an 8-bit field within the operation word. The data is sign-extended to a long operand and all 32 bits are transferred to the data register.

Condition Codes:

X	N	Z	V	C
—	*	*	0	0

N　Set if the result is negative. Cleared otherwise.
Z　Set if the result is zero. Cleared otherwise.
V　Always cleared.
C　Always cleared.
X　Not affected.

Instruction Format:

15	14	13	12	11 10 9	8	7 6 5 4 3 2 1 0
0	1	1	1	Register	0	Data

Instruction Fields:

Register field — Specifies the data register to be loaded.
Data field — 8 bits of data which are sign extended to a long operand.

MOVES

MOVES

Operation: If supervisor state
then Rn → Destination <DFC>
Source <SFC> → Rn
else TRAP

Assembler   MOVES Rn, <ea>
Syntax: MOVES <ea>, Rn

Attributes: Size = (Byte, Word, Long)

Description: Move the byte, word, or long operand from the specified general register to a location within the address space specified by the destination function code (DFC) register. Or, move the byte, word, or long operand from a location within the address space specified by the source function code (SFC) register to the specified general register.

    If the destination is a data register, the source operand replaces the corresponding low-order bits of the that data register. If the destination is an address register, the source operand is sign-extended to 32 bits and then loaded into that address register.

Condition Codes: Not affected.

Instruction Format:

15	14	13	12	11	10	9	8	7	6	5	4	3	2	1	0
0	0	0	0	1	1	1	0	Size		Effective Address					
A/D	Register		dr	0	0	0	0	0	0	0	0	0	0	0	0

Instruction Fields:

Size field — Specifies the size of the operation:
00—byte operation.
01—word operation.
10—long operation.

A/D field — Specifies the type of general register:
0—data register.
1—address register.
Register field — Specifies the register number.
dr field — Specifies the direction of the transfer:
0—from <ea> to general register.
1—from general register to <ea>.

—Continued—

MC68010

MOVES

MOVES

Instruction Fields: (continued)

Effective Address field — Specifies the source or destination location within the alternate address space. Only alterable memory addressing modes are allowed as shown:

Addressing Mode	Mode	Register
Dn	—	—
An	—	—
(An)	010	register number
(An) +	011	register number
− (An)	100	register number
d(An)	101	register number

Addressing Mode	Mode	Register
d(An, Xi)	110	register number
Abs.W	111	000
Abs.L	111	001
d(PC)	—	—
d(PC, Xi)	—	—
Imm	—	—

MC68010

123

MULS

Signed Multiply

MULS

Operation: (Source)*(Destination)→ Destination

**Assembler
Syntax:** MULS <ea>, Dn

Attributes: Size = (Word)

Description: Multiply two signed 16-bit operands yielding a 32-bit signed result. The operation is performed using signed arithmetic. A register operand is taken from the low order word; the upper word is unused. All 32 bits of the product are saved in the destination data register.

Condition Codes:

X	N	Z	V	C
—	*	*	0	0

N Set if the result is negative. Cleared otherwise.
Z Set if the result is zero. Cleared otherwise.
V Always cleared.
C Always cleared.
X Not affected.

Instruction Format:

15	14	13	12	11 10 9	8	7	6	5 4 3	2 1 0
1	1	0	0	Register	1	1	1	Effective Address Mode	Register

Instruction Fields:

Register field — Specifies one of the data registers. This field always specifies the destination.

Effective Address field — Specifies the source operand. Only data addressing modes are allowed as shown:

Addressing Mode	Mode	Register	Addressing Mode	Mode	Register
Dn	000	register number	d(An, Xi)	110	register number
An	—	—	Abs.W	111	000
(An)	010	register number	Abs.L	111	001
(An) +	011	register number	d(PC)	111	010
– (An)	100	register number	d(PC, Xi)	111	011
d(An)	101	register number	Imm	111	100

MULU   Unsigned Mulitply   # MULU

Operation: (Source)*(Destination)→ Destination

**Assembler
Syntax:**   MULU <ea>, Dn

Attributes: Size = (Word)

Description: Multiply two unsigned 16-bit operands yielding a 32-bit unsigned result. The
operation is performed using unsigned arithmetic. A register operand is
taken from the low order word; the upper word is unused. All 32 bits of the
product are saved in the destination data register.

Condition Codes:

X	N	Z	V	C
—	*	*	0	0

N   Set if the most significant bit of the result is set. Cleared otherwise.
Z   Set if the result is zero. Cleared otherwise.
V   Always cleared.
C   Always cleared.
X   Not affected.

Instruction Format:

15	14	13	12	11	10	9	8	7	6	5	4	3	2	1	0
1	1	0	0	Register			0	1	1	Effective Address Mode / Register					

Instruction Fields:

Register field — Specifies one of the data registers. This field always specifies the destination.

Effective Address field — Specifies the source operand. Only data addressing modes are allowed as shown:

Addressing Mode	Mode	Register	Addressing Mode	Mode	Register
Dn	000	register number	d(An, Xi)	110	register number
An	—	—	Abs.W	111	000
(An)	010	register number	Abs.L	111	001
(An)+	011	register number	d(PC)	111	010
−(An)	100	register number	d(PC, Xi)	111	011
d(An)	101	register number	Imm	111	100

NBCD

Negate Decimal with Extend

NBCD

Operation: $0 - (Destination)_{10} - X \rightarrow Destination$

**Assembler
Syntax:** NBCD <ea>

Attributes: Size = (Byte)

Description: The operand addressed as the destination and the extend bit are sub-tracted from zero. The operation is performed using decimal arithmetic. The result is saved in the destination location. This instruction produces the tens complement of the destination if the extend bit is clear, the nines complement if the extend bit is set. This is a byte operation only.

Condition Codes:

X	N	Z	V	C
*	U	*	U	*

N   Undefined.
Z   Cleared if the result is non-zero. Unchanged otherwise.
V   Undefined.
C   Set if a borrow (decimal) was generated. Cleared otherwise.
X   Set the same as the carry bit.

NOTE

Normally the Z condition code bit is set via programming before the start of an operation. This allows successful tests for zero results upon completion of multiple-precision operations.

Instruction Format:

15	14	13	12	11	10	9	8	7	6	5	4	3	2	1	0
0	1	0	0	1	0	0	0	0	0	Effective Address Mode | Register				

Instruction Fields:

Effective Address field — Specifies the destination operand. Only data alterable addressing modes are allowed as shown:

Addressing Mode	Mode	Register	Addressing Mode	Mode	Register
Dn	000	register number	d(An, Xi)	110	register number
An	—	—	Abs.W	111	000
(An)	010	register number	Abs.L	111	001
(An) +	011	register number	d(PC)	—	—
− (An)	100	register number	d(PC, Xi)	—	—
d(An)	101	register number	Imm	—	—

NEG   Negate   NEG

Operation: 0 − (Destination) → Destination

Assembler
Syntax: NEG <ea>

Attributes: Size = (Byte, Word, Long)

Description: The operand addressed as the destination is subtracted from zero. The result is stored in the destination location. The size of the operation may be specified to be byte, word, or long.

Condition Codes:

X	N	Z	V	C
*	*	*	*	*

N   Set if the result is negative. Cleared otherwise.
Z   Set if the result is zero. Cleared otherwise.
V   Set if an overflow is generated. Cleared otherwise.
C   Cleared if the result is zero. Set otherwise.
X   Set the same as the carry bit.

Instruction Format:

15	14	13	12	11	10	9	8	7	6	5	4	3	2	1	0
0	1	0	0	0	1	0	0	Size		Effective Address Mode | Register					

Instruction Fields:

Size field — Specifies the size of the operation:
   00 — byte operation.
   01 — word operation.
   10 — long operation.

Effective Address field — Specifies the destination operand. Only data alterable addressing modes are allowed as shown:

Addressing Mode	Mode	Register	Addressing Mode	Mode	Register
Dn	000	register number	d(An, Xi)	110	register number
An	—	—	Abs.W	111	000
(An)	010	register number	Abs.L	111	001
(An) +	011	register number	d(PC)	—	—
− (An)	100	register number	d(PC, Xi)	—	—
d(An)	101	register number	Imm	—	—

NEGX

Negate with Extend

NEGX

Operation: 0 – (Destination) – X → Destination

**Assembler
Syntax:** NEGX <ea>

Attributes: Size = (Byte, Word, Long)

Description: The operand addressed as the destination and the extend bit are sub-
tracted from zero. The result is stored in the destination location. The size
of the operation may be specified to be byte, word, or long.

Condition Codes:

X	N	Z	V	C
*	*	*	*	*

N   Set if the result is negative. Cleared otherwise.
Z   Cleared if the result is non-zero. Unchanged otherwise.
V   Set if an overflow is generated. Cleared otherwise.
C   Set if a borrow is generated. Cleared otherwise.
X   Set the same as the carry bit.

NOTE
Normally the Z condition code bit is set via programming
before the start of an operation. This allows successful
tests for zero results upon completion of multiple-
precision operations.

Instruction Format:

15	14	13	12	11	10	9	8	7	6	5	4	3	2	1	0
0	1	0	0	0	0	0	0	Size		Effective Address Mode | Register					

Instruction Fields:

Size field — Specifies the size of the operation:
00 — byte operation.
01 — word operation.
10 — long operation.

Effective Address field — Specifies the destination operand. Only data
alterable addressing modes are allowed as shown:

Addressing Mode	Mode	Register	Addressing Mode	Mode	Register
Dn	000	register number	d(An, Xi)	110	register number
An	—	—	Abs.W	111	000
(An)	010	register number	Abs.L	111	001
(An) +	011	register number	d(PC)	—	—
– (An)	100	register number	d(PC, Xi)	—	—
d(An)	101	register number	Imm	—	—

NOP

No Operation

NOP

Operation: None

**Assembler
Syntax:** NOP

Attributes: Unsized

Description: No operation occurs. The processor state, other than the program counter, is unaffected. Execution continues with the instruction following the NOP instruction.

Condition Codes: Not affected.

Instruction Format:

15	14	13	12	11	10	9	8	7	6	5	4	3	2	1	0
0	1	0	0	1	1	1	0	0	1	1	1	0	0	0	1

NOT

Logical Complement

NOT

Operation: ~(Destination) → Destination

Assembler
Syntax: NOT <ea>

Attributes: Size = (Byte, Word, Long)

Description: The ones complement of the destination operand is taken and the result stored in the destination location. The size of the operation may be specified to be byte, word, or long.

Condition Codes:

```
X  N  Z  V  C
—  *  *  0  0
```

N   Set if the result is negative. Cleared otherwise.
Z   Set if the result is zero. Cleared otherwise.
V   Always cleared.
C   Always cleared.
X   Not affected.

Instruction Format:

15	14	13	12	11	10	9	8	7	6	5	4	3	2	1	0
0	1	0	0	0	1	1	0	Size		Effective Address Mode | Register					

Instruction Fields:

Size field — Specifies the size of the operation:
00 — byte operation.
01 — word operation.
10 — long operation.

Effective Address field — Specifies the destination operand. Only data alterable addressing modes are allowed as shown:

Addressing Mode	Mode	Register	Addressing Mode	Mode	Register
Dn	000	register number	d(An, Xi)	110	register number
An	—	—	Abs.W	111	000
(An)	010	register number	Abs.L	111	001
(An)+	011	register number	d(PC)	—	—
−(An)	100	register number	d(PC, Xi)	—	—
d(An)	101	register number	Imm	—	—

130

OR

Inclusive OR Logical

OR

Operation: (Source) v (Destination)→ Destination

Assembler OR <ea>, Dn
Syntax: OR Dn, <ea>

Attributes: Size = (Byte, Word, Long)

Description: Inclusive OR the source operand to the destination operand and store the result in the destination location. The size of the operation may be specified to be byte, word, or long. The contents of an address register may not be used as an operand.

Condition Codes:

X	N	Z	V	C
—	*	*	0	0

N   Set if the most significant bit of the result is set. Cleared otherwise.
Z   Set if the result is zero. Cleared otherwise.
V   Always cleared.
C   Always cleared.
X   Not affected.

Instruction Format:

15	14	13	12	11 10 9	8 7 6	5 4 3	2 1 0
1	0	0	0	Register	Op-Mode	Effective Address Mode	Register

Instruction Fields:

Register field — Specifies any of the eight data registers.
Op-Mode field —

Byte	Word	Long	Operation
000	001	010	(<Dn>) v (<ea>)→ <Dn>
100	101	110	(<ea>) v (<Dn>)→ <ea>

Effective Address field —
   If the location specified is a source operand then only data addressing modes are allowed as shown:

Addressing Mode	Mode	Register	Addressing Mode	Mode	Register
Dn	000	register number	d(An, Xi)	110	register number
An	—	—	Abs.W	111	000
(An)	010	register number	Abs.L	111	001
(An)+	011	register number	d(PC)	111	010
−(An)	100	register number	d(PC, Xi)	111	011
d(An)	101	register number	Imm	111	100

— Continued —

OR

OR

Effective Address field (Continued)

If the location specified is a destination operand then only memory alterable addressing modes are allowed as shown:

Addressing Mode	Mode	Register	Addressing Mode	Mode	Register
Dn	—	—	d(An, Xi)	110	register number
An	—	—	Abs.W	111	000
(An)	010	register number	Abs.L	111	001
(An)+	011	register number	d(PC)	—	—
−(An)	100	register number	d(PC, Xi)	—	—
d(An)	101	register number	Imm	—	—

Notes: 1. If the destination is a data register, then it cannot be specified by using the destination <ea> mode, but must use the destination Dn mode instead.
2. ORI is used when the source is immediate data. Most assemblers automatically make this distinction.

ORI

Inclusive OR Immediate

ORI

Operation: Immediate Data v (Destination) → Destination

**Assembler
Syntax:** ORI #<data>, <ea>

Attributes: Size = (Byte, Word, Long)

Description: Inclusive OR the immediate data to the destination operand and store the result in the destination location. The size of the operation may be specified to be byte, word, or long. The size of the immediate data matches the operation size.

Condition Codes:

X	N	Z	V	C
—	*	*	0	0

N   Set if the most significant bit of the result is set. Cleared otherwise.
Z   Set if the result is zero. Cleared otherwise.
V   Always cleared.
C   Always cleared.
X   Not affected.

Instruction Format:

15	14	13	12	11	10	9	8	7	6	5	4	3	2	1	0
0	0	0	0	0	0	0	0	Size		Effective Address Mode | Register					
Word Data (16 bites)								Byte Data (8 bits)							
Long Data (32 bits, including previous word)															

Instruction Fields:

Size field — Specifies the size of the operation:
00 — byte operation.
01 — word operation.
10 — long operation.

Effective Address field — Specifies the destination operand. Only data alterable addressing modes are allowed as shown:

Addressing Mode	Mode	Register	Addressing Mode	Mode	Register
Dn	000	register number	d(An, Xi)	110	register number
An	—	—	Abs.W	111	000
(An)	010	register number	Abs.L	111	001
(An)+	011	register number	d(PC)	—	—
−(An)	100	register number	d(PC, Xi)	—	—
d(An)	101	register number	Imm	—	—

Immediate field — (Data immediately following the instruction):
If size = 00, then the data is the low order byte of the immediate word.
If size = 01, then the data is the entire immediate word.
If size = 10, then the data is the next two immediate words.

133

ORI
to CCR

ORI
to CCR

Operation: (Source) v CCR → CCR

Assembler
Syntax: ORI #xxx, CCR

Attributes: Size = (Byte)

Description: Inclusive OR the immediate operand with the condition codes and store the result in the low-order byte of the status register.

Condition Codes:

X	N	Z	V	C
*	*	*	*	*

N Set if bit 3 of immediate operand is one. Unchanged otherwise.
Z Set if bit 2 of immediate operand is one. Unchanged otherwise.
V Set if bit 1 of immediate operand is one. Unchanged otherwise.
C Set if bit 0 of immediate operand is one. Unchanged otherwise.
X Set if bit 4 of immediate operand is one. Unchanged otherwise.

Instruction Format:

15	14	13	12	11	10	9	8	7	6	5	4	3	2	1	0
0	0	0	0	0	0	0	0	0	0	1	1	1	1	0	0
0	0	0	0	0	0	0	0	Byte Data (8 bits)							

ORI
to SR

ORI
to SR

Inclusive OR Immediate to the Status Register
(Privileged Instruction)

Operation: If supervisor state
           then (Source) v SR → SR
           else TRAP

Assembler
Syntax: ORI #xxx, SR

Attributes: Size = (Word)

Description: Inclusive OR the immediate operand with the contents of the status register and store the result in the status register. All bits of the status register are affected.

Condition Codes:

X N Z V C

*	*	*	*	*

N   Set if bit 3 of immediate operand is one. Unchanged otherwise.
Z   Set if bit 2 of immediate operand is one. Unchanged otherwise.
V   Set if bit 1 of immediate operand is one. Unchanged otherwise.
C   Set if bit 0 of immediate operand is one. Unchanged otherwise.
X   Set if bit 4 of immediate operand is one. Unchanged otherwise.

Instruction Format:

15	14	13	12	11	10	9	8	7	6	5	4	3	2	1	0
0	0	0	0	0	0	0	0	0	1	1	1	1	1	0	0
Word Data (16 bits)															

135

PEA

Push Effective Address

PEA

Operation: Destination → − (SP)

**Assembler
Syntax:** PEA < ea >

Attributes: Size = (Long)

Description: The effective address is computed and pushed onto the stack. A long word address is pushed onto the stack.

Condition Codes: Not affected.

Instruction Format:

15	14	13	12	11	10	9	8	7	6	5 4 3	2 1 0
0	1	0	0	1	0	0	0	0	1	Effective Address Mode	Register

Instruction Fields:

Effective Address field — Specifies the address to be pushed onto the stack. Only control addressing modes are allowed as shown:

Addressing Mode	Mode	Register	Addressing Mode	Mode	Register
Dn	—	—	d(An, Xi)	110	register number
An	—	—	Abs.W	111	000
(An)	010	register number	Abs.L	111	001
(An) +	—	—	d(PC)	111	010
− (An)	—	—	d(PC, Xi)	111	011
d(An)	101	register number	Imm	—	—

RESET

Reset External Devices
(Privileged Instruction)

Operation: If supervisor state
             then Assert RESET Line
             else TRAP

Assembler
Syntax: RESET

Attributes: Unsized

Description: The reset line is asserted causing all external devices to be reset. The processor state, other than the program counter, is unaffected and execution continues with the next instruction.

Condition Codes: Not affected.

Instruction Format:

15	14	13	12	11	10	9	8	7	6	5	4	3	2	1	0
0	1	0	0	1	1	1	0	0	1	1	1	0	0	0	0

Rotate (without Extend)

Operation: (Destination) Rotated by <count> → Destination

Assembler   ROd Dx, Dy
Syntax: ROd #<data>, Dy
ROd <ea>

Attributes: Size = (Byte, Word, Long)

Description: Rotate the bits of the operand in the direction specified. The extend bit is not included in the rotation. The shift count for the rotation of a register may be specified in two different ways:
1. Immediate — the shift count is specified in the instruction (shift range, 1-8).
2. Register — the shift count is contained in a data register specified in the instruction.

The size of the operation may be specified to be byte, word, or long. The content of memory may be rotated one bit only and the operand size is restricted to a word.

For ROL, the operand is rotated left; the number of positions shifted is the shift count. Bits shifted out of the high order bit go to both the carry bit and back into the low order bit. The extend bit is not modified or used.

ROL:

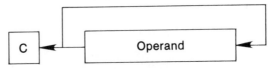

For ROR, the operand is rotated right; the number of position shifted is the shift count. Bits shifted out of the low order bit go to both the carry bit and back into the high order bit. The extend bit is not modified or used.

ROR:

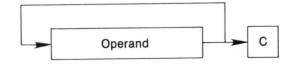

Condition Codes:

X	N	Z	V	C
—	*	*	0	*

N   Set if the most significant bit of the result is set. Cleared otherwise.
Z   Set if the result is zero. Cleared otherwise.
V   Always cleared.
C   Set according to the last bit shfited out of the operand. Cleared for a shift count of zero.
X   Not affected.

— Continued —

ROL
ROR

Rotate (Without Extend)

ROL
ROR

Instruction Format (Register Rotate):

15	14	13	12	11	10	9	8	7	6	5	4	3	2	1	0
1	1	1	0	Count/Register			dr	Size		i/r	1	1	Register		

Instruction Fields (Register Rotate):

Count/Register field —
> if i/r = 0, the rotate count is specified in this field. The values 0, 1-7 represent a range of 8, 1 to 7 respectively.
> If i/r = 1, the rotate count (modulo 64) is contained in the data register specified in this field.

dr field — Specifies the direction of the rotate:
> 0 — rotate right.
> 1 — rotate left.

Size field — Specifies the size of the operation:
> 00 — byte operation.
> 01 — word operation.
> 10 — long operation.

i/r field —
> If i/r = 0, specifies immediate rotate count.
> If i/r = 1, specifies register rotate count.

Register field — Specifies a data register whose content is to be rotated.

Instruction Format (Memory Rotate):

15	14	13	12	11	10	9	8	7	6	5	4	3	2	1	0
1	1	1	0	0	1	1	dr	1	1	Effective Address Mode			Register		

Instruction Fields (Memory Rotate):

dr field — Specifies the direction of the rotate:
> 0 — rotate right
> 1 — rotate left

Effective Address field — Specifies the operand to be rotated. Only memory alterable addressing modes are allowed as shown:

Addressing Mode	Mode	Register	Addressing Mode	Mode	Register
Dn	—	—	d(An, Xi)	110	register number
An	—	—	Abs.W	111	000
(An)	010	register number	Abs.L	111	001
(An)+	011	register number	d(PC)	—	—
−(An)	100	register number	d(PC, Xi)	—	—
d(An)	101	register number	Imm	—	—

ROXL ROXR

Rotate with Extend

ROXL ROXR

Operation: (Destination) Rotated by <count> → Destination

Assembler Syntax:
ROXd Dx, Dy
ROXd #<data>, Dy
ROXd <ea>

Attributes: Size = (Byte, Word, Long)

Description: Rotate the bits of the destination operand in the direction specified. The extend bit is included in the rotation. The shift count for the rotation of a register may be specified in two different ways:
1. Immediate — the shift count is specified in the instruction (shift range, 1-8).
2. Register — the shift count is contained in a data register specified in the instruction.
The size of the operation may be specified to be byte, word, or long. The content of memory may be rotated one bit only and the operand size is restricted to a word.

For ROXL, the operand is rotated left; the number of positions shifted is the shift count. Bits shifted out of the high order bit go to both the carry and extend bits; the previous value of the extend bit is shifted into the low order bit.

ROXL:

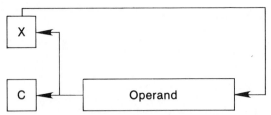

For ROXR, the operand is rotated right; the number of positions shifted is the shift count. Bits shifted out of the low order bit go to both the carry and extend bits; the previous value of the extend bit is shifted into the high order bit.

ROXR:

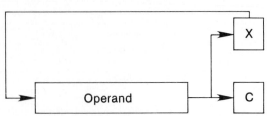

— Continued —

ROXL
ROXR

Rotate with Extend

ROXL
ROXR

Condition Codes:

X	N	Z	V	C
*	*	*	0	*

N   Set if the most significant bit of the result is set. Cleared otherwise.
Z   Set if the result is zero. Cleared otherwise.
V   Always cleared.
C   Set according to the last bit shifted out of the operand. Set to the value of the extend bit for a shift count of zero.
X   Set according to the last bit shifted out of the operand. Unaffected for a shift count of zero.

Instruction Format (Register Rotate):

15	14	13	12	11 10 9	8	7 6	5	4	3	2 1 0
1	1	1	0	Count/ Register	dr	Size	i/r	1	0	Register

Instruction Fields (Register Rotate):

Count/Register field:

If i/r = 0, the rotate count is specified in this field. The values 0, 1-7 represent range of 8, 1 to 7 respectively.

If i/r = 1, the rotate count (modulo 64) is contained in the data register specified in this field.

dr field — Specifies the direction of the rotate:

0 — rotate right.
1 — rotate left.

Size field — Specifies the size of the operation:

00 — byte operation.
01 — word operation.
10 — long operation.

i/r field —

If i/r = 0, specifies immediate rotate count.
If i/r = 1, specifies register rotate count.

Register field — Specifies a data register whose content is to be rotated.

— Continued —

ROXL
ROXR

Rotate with Extend

ROXL
ROXR

Instruction Format (Memory Rotate):

15	14	13	12	11	10	9	8	7	6	5	4	3	2	1	0
1	1	1	0	0	1	0	dr	1	1	Effective Address Mode			Register		

Instruction Fields (Memory Rotate):

dr field — Specifies the direction of the rotate:

0 — rotate right.

1 — rotate left.

Effective Address field — Specifies the operand to be rotated. Only memory alterable addressing modes are allowed as shown:

Addressing Mode	Mode	Register	Addressing Mode	Mode	Register
Dn	—	—	d(An, Xi)	110	register number
An	—	—	Abs.W	111	000
(An)	010	register number	Abs.L	111	001
(An)+	011	register number	d(PC)	—	—
−(An)	100	register number	d(PC, Xi)	—	—
d(An)	101	register number	Imm	—	—

142

RTD

Return and Deallocate Parameters

Operation: (SP) + →PC; SP + d→SP

Assembler
Syntax: RTD #<displacement>

Attributes: Unsized

Description: The program counter is pulled from the stack. The previous program counter value is lost. After the program counter is read from the stack, the displacement value is sign-extended to 32 bits and added to the stack pointer.

Condition Codes: Not affected.

Instruction Format:

15	14	13	12	11	10	9	8	7	6	5	4	3	2	1	0
0	1	0	0	1	1	1	0	0	1	1	1	0	1	0	0
Displacement															

Instruction Field:

Displacement field — Specifies the twos complement integer which is to be sign-extended and added to the stack pointer.

RTE

Return from Exception
(Privileged Instruction)

RTE

Operation: If supervisor state
  then (SP)+ → SR; (SP)+ → PC
  else TRAP

Assembler
Syntax: RTE

Attributes: Unsized

Description: The status register and program counter are pulled from the system stack. The previous status register and program counter are lost. All bits in the status register are affected.

Condition Codes: Set according to the content of the word on the stack.

Instruction Format:

15	14	13	12	11	10	9	8	7	6	5	4	3	2	1	0
0	1	0	0	1	1	1	0	0	1	1	1	0	0	1	1

RTE

Return from Exception
(Privileged Instruction)

RTE

Operation: If supervisor state
  then (SP) + → SR; (SP) + → PC
   If (SP) + = long format
     then full restore
   else TRAP

Assembler
Syntax: RTE

Attributes: Unsized

Description: The status register and program counter are pulled from the system stack. The previous status register and program counter are lost. The vector offset word is also pulled from the stack and the format field is examined to determine the amount of information to be restored.

Condition Codes: Set according to the content of the word on the stack.

Instruction Format:

15	14	13	12	11	10	9	8	7	6	5	4	3	2	1	0
0	1	0	0	1	1	1	0	0	1	1	1	0	0	1	1

Vector Offset Word Format:

15			12	11	10	9								0
Format				0	0	Vector Offset								

Vector Offset Word Format Fields:
  Format Field: — Specifies the amount of information to be restored.
    0000 — Short. Four words are to be removed from the top of the stack.
    1000 — Long. Twenty-nine words are to be removed from the top of the stack.
  Any Other
    Pattern — Error. The processor takes the format error exception.

RTR

Return and Restore Condition Codes

RTR

Operation: $(SP)+ \rightarrow CC; (SP)+ \rightarrow PC$

**Assembler
Syntax:** RTR

Attributes: Unsized

Description: The condition codes and program counter are pulled from the stack. The previous condition codes and program counter are lost. The supervisor portion of the status register is unaffected.

Condition Codes: Set according to the content of the word on the stack.

Instruction Format:

15	14	13	12	11	10	9	8	7	6	5	4	3	2	1	0
0	1	0	0	1	1	1	0	0	1	1	1	0	1	1	1

RTS

Return from Subroutine

RTS

Operation: $(SP) + \rightarrow PC$

**Assembler
Syntax:** RTS

Attributes: Unsized

Description: The program counter is pulled from the stack. The previous program counter is lost.

Condition Codes: Not affected.

Instruction Format:

15	14	13	12	11	10	9	8	7	6	5	4	3	2	1	0
0	1	0	0	1	1	1	0	0	1	1	1	0	1	0	1

SBCD

Subtract Decimal with Extend

SBCD

Operation: $(Destination)_{10} - (Source)_{10} - X \rightarrow Destination$

Assembler
Syntax: SBCD Dy, Dx
SBCD $-(Ay)$, $-(Ax)$

Attributes: Size = (Byte)

Description: Subtract the source operand from the destination operand along with the extend bit and store the result in the destination location. The subtraction is performed using binary coded decimal arithmetic. The operands may be addressed in two different ways:
1. Data register to data register: The operands are contained in the data registers specified in the instruction.
2. Memory to memory: The operands are addressed with the predecrement addressing mode using the address registers specified in the instruction.

This operation is a byte operation only.

Condition Codes:

X	N	Z	V	C
*	U	*	U	*

N   Undefined.
Z   Cleared if the result is non-zero. Unchanged otherwise.
V   Undefined.
C   Set if a borrow (decimal) is generated. Cleared otherwise.
X   Set the same as the carry bit.

NOTE
Normally the Z condition code bit is set via programming before the start of an operation. This allows successful tests for zero results upon completion of multiple-precision operations.

Instruction Format:

15	14	13	12	11 10 9	8	7	6	5	4	3	2 1 0
1	0	0	0	Register Rx	1	0	0	0	0	R/M	Register Ry

Instruction Fields:

Register Rx field — Specifies the destination register:
If R/M = 0, specifies a data register.
If R/M = 1, specifies an address register for the prececrement addressing mode.
R/M field — Specifies the operand addressing mode:
0 — The operation is data register to data register.
1 — The operation is memory to memory.
Register Ry field — Specifies the source register:
If R/M = 0, specifies a data register.
If R/M = 1, specifies an address register for the predecrement addressing mode.

Set According to Condition

Operation: If (Condition True)
then 1s → Destination
else 0s → Destination

**Assembler
Syntax:** Scc <ea>

Attributes: Size = (Byte)

Description: The specified condition code is tested; if the condition is true, the byte specified by the effective address is set to TRUE (all ones), otherwise that byte is set to FALSE (all zeroes). "cc" may specify the following conditions:

CC	carry clear	0100	$\overline{C}$	LS	low or same	0011	$C + Z$
CS	carry set	0101	C	LT	less than	1101	$N \cdot \overline{V} + \overline{N} \cdot V$
EQ	equal	0111	Z	MI	minus	1011	N
F	false	0001	0	NE	not equal	0110	$\overline{Z}$
GE	greater or equal	1100	$N \cdot V + \overline{N} \cdot \overline{V}$	PI	plus	1010	$\overline{N}$
GT	greater than	1110	$N \cdot V \cdot \overline{Z} + \overline{N} \cdot \overline{V} \cdot \overline{Z}$	T	true	0000	1
HI	high	0010	$\overline{C} \cdot \overline{Z}$	VC	overflow clear	1000	$\overline{V}$
LE	less or equal	1111	$Z + N \cdot \overline{V} + \overline{N} \cdot V$	VS	overflow set	1001	V

Condition Codes: Not affected.

Instruction Format:

15	14	13	12	11	10	9	8	7	6	5	4	3	2	1	0
0	1	0	1	Condition				1	1	Effective Address					
										Mode			Register		

Instruction Fields:

Condition field — One of sixteen conditions discussed in description.

Effective Address field — Specifies the location in which the true/false byte is to be stored. Only data alterable addressing modes are allowed as shown:

Addressing Mode	Mode	Register	Addressing Mode	Mode	Register
Dn	000	register number	d(An, Xi)	110	register number
An	—	—	Abs.W	111	000
(An)	010	register number	Abs.L	111	001
(An) +	011	register number	d(PC)	—	—
− (An)	100	register number	d(PC, Xi)	—	—
d(An)	101	register number	Imm	—	—

Notes:
1. A memory destination is read before being written to.
2. An arithmetic one and zero result may be generated by following the Scc instruction with a NEG instruction.

STOP

Load Status Register and Stop
(Privileged Instruction)

Operation: If supervisor state
then Immediate Data → SR; STOP
else TRAP

Assembler
Syntax: STOP #xxx

Attributes: Unsized

Description: The immediate operand is moved into the entire status register; the program counter is advanced to point to the next instruction and the processor stops fetching and executing instructions. Execution of instructions resumes when a trace, interrupt, or reset exception occurs. A trace exception will occur if the trace state is on when the STOP instruction is executed. If an interrupt request arrives whose priority is higher than the current processor priority, an interrupt exception occurs, otherwise the interrupt request has no effect. If the bit of the immediate data corresponding to the S-bit is off, execution of the instruction will cause a privilege violation. External reset will always initiate reset exception processing.

Condition Codes: Set according to the immediate operand.

Instruction Format:

15	14	13	12	11	10	9	8	7	6	5	4	3	2	1	0
0	1	0	0	1	1	1	0	0	1	1	1	0	0	1	0
Immediate Data															

Instruction Fields:
Immediate field — Specifies the data to be loaded into the status register.

150

SUB

Subtract Binary

SUB

Operation: (Destination) – (Source) → Destination

Assembler SUB <ea>, Dn
Syntax: SUB Dn, <ea>

Attributes: Size = (Byte, Word, Long)

Description: Subtract the source operand from the destination operand and store the result in the destination. The size of the operation may be specified to be byte, word, or long. The mode of the instruction indicates which operand is the source and which is the destination as well as the operand size.

Condition Codes:

X	N	Z	V	C
*	*	*	*	*

N Set if the result is negative. Cleared otherwise.
Z Set if the result is zero. Cleared otherwise.
V Set if an overflow is generated. Cleared otherwise.
C Set if a borrow is generated. Cleared otherwise.
X Set the same as the carry bit.

Instruction Format:

15	14	13	12	11 10 9	8 7 6	5 4 3	2 1 0
1	0	0	1	Register	Op-Mode	Effective Address Mode	Register

Instruction Fields:

Register field — Specifies any of the eight data registers.
Op-Mode field —

Byte	Word	Long	Operation
000	001	010	(<Dn>)–(<ea>)→ <Dn>
100	101	110	(<ea>)–(<Dn>)→ <ea>

Effective Address field — Determines addressing mode:
If the location specified is a source operand, then all addressing modes are allowed as shown:

Addressing Mode	Mode	Register	Addressing Mode	Mode	Register
Dn	000	register number	d(An, Xi)	110	register number
An*	001	register number	Abs.W	111	000
(An)	010	register number	Abs.L	111	001
(An)+	011	register number	d(PC)	111	010
–(An)	100	register number	d(PC, Xi)	111	011
d(An)	101	register number	Imm	111	100

*For byte size operation, address register direct is not allowed.

— Continued —

Effective Address field (Continued)

If the location specified is a destination operand, then only alterable memory addressing modes are allowed as shown:

Addressing Mode	Mode	Register	Addressing Mode	Mode	Register
Dn	—	—	d(An, Xi)	110	register number
An	—	—	Abs.W	111	000
(An)	010	register number	Abs.L	111	001
(An) +	011	register number	d(PC)	—	—
– (An)	100	register number	d(PC, Xi)	—	—
d(An)	101	register number	Imm	—	—

Notes:
1. If the destination is a data register, then it cannot be specified by using the destination <ea> mode, but must use the destination Dn mode instead.
2. SUBA is used when the destination is an address register. SUBI and SUBQ are used when the source is immediate data. Most assemblers automatically make this distinction.

SUBA

Subtract Address

SUBA

Operation: (Destination) − (Source) → Destination

Assembler
Syntax: SUBA <ea>, An

Attributes: Size = (Word, Long)

Description: Subtract the source operand from the destination address register and store the result in the address register. The size of the operation may be specified to be word or long. Word size source operands are sign extended to 32 bit quantities before the operation is done.

Condition Codes: Not affected.

Instruction Format:

15	14	13	12	11 10 9	8 7 6	5 4 3	2 1 0
1	0	0	1	Register	Op-Mode	Effective Address Mode	Register

Instruction Fields:

Register field — Specifies any of the eight address registers. This is always the destination.

Op-Mode field — Specifies the size of the operation:

011 — Word operation. The source operand is sign-extended to a long operand and the operation is performed on the address register using all 32 bits.

111 — Long operations.

Effective Address field — Specifies the source operand. All addressing modes are allowed as shown:

Addressing Mode	Mode	Register	Addressing Mode	Mode	Register
Dn	000	register number	d(An, Xi)	110	register number
An	001	register number	Abs.W	111	000
(An)	010	register number	Abs.L	111	001
(An)+	011	register number	d(PC)	111	010
−(An)	100	register number	d(PC, Xi)	111	011
d(An)	101	register number	Imm	111	100

SUBI

Subtract Immediate

SUBI

Operation: (Destination) – Immediate Data → Destination

**Assembler
Syntax:** SUBI #<data>, <ea>

Attributes: Size = (Byte, Word, Long)

Description: Subtract the immediate data from the destination operand and store the result in the destination location. The size of the operation may be specified to be byte, word, or long. The size of the immediate data matches the operation size.

Condition Codes:

X	N	Z	V	C
*	*	*	*	*

N   Set if the result is negative. Cleared otherwise.
Z   Set if the result is zero. Cleared otherwise.
V   Set if an overflow is generated. Cleared otherwise.
C   Set if a borrow is generated. Cleared otherwise.
X   Set the same as the carry bit.

Instruction Format:

15	14	13	12	11	10	9	8	7	6	5	4	3	2	1	0
0	0	0	0	0	1	0	0	Size		Effective Address					
										Mode			Register		
Word Data (16 bits)								Byte Data (8 bits)							
Long Data (32 bits, including previous word)															

Instruction Fields:

Size field — Specifies the size of the operation.
00 — byte operation.
01 — word operation.
10 — long operation.

Effective Address field — Specifies the destination operand. Only data alterable addressing modes are allowed as shown:

Addressing Mode	Mode	Register	Addressing Mode	Mode	Register
Dn	000	register number	d(An, Xi)	110	register number
An	—	—	Abs.W	111	000
(An)	010	register number	Abs.L	111	001
(An)+	011	register number	d(PC)	—	—
–(An)	100	register number	d(PC, Xi)	—	—
d(An)	101	register number	Imm	—	—

Immediate field — (Data immediately following the instruction)
If size = 00, then the data is the low order byte of the immediate word.
If size = 01, then the data is the entire immediate word.
If size = 10, then the data is the next two immediate words.

SUBQ

Subtract Quick

SUBQ

Operation: (Destination) – Immediate Data → Destination

**Assembler
Syntax:** SUBQ #<data>, <ea>

Attributes: Size = (Byte, Word, Long)

Description: Subtract the immediate data from the destination operand. The data range is from 1-8. The size of the operation may be specified to be byte, word, or long. Word and long operations are also allowed on the address registers and the condition codes are not affected. Word size source operands are sign extended to 32 bit quantities before the operation is done.

Condition Codes:

X	N	Z	V	C
*	*	*	*	*

N   Set if the result is negative. Cleared otherwise.
Z   Set if the result is zero. Cleared otherwise.
V   Set if an overflow is generated. Cleared otherwise.
C   Set if a borrow is generated. Cleared otherwise.
X   Set the same as the carry bit.

The condition codes are not affected if a subtraction from an address register is made.

Instruction Format:

15	14	13	12	11	10	9	8	7	6	5 4 3	2 1 0
0	1	0	1		Data		1		Size	Effective Address Mode	Register

Instruction Fields:

Data field — Three bits of immediate data, 0, 1-7 representing a range of 8, 1 to 7 respectively.
Size field — Specifies the size of the operation:
   00 — byte operation.
   01 — word operation.
   10 — long operation.
Effective Address field — Specifies the destination location. Only alterable addressing modes are allowed as shown:

Addressing Mode	Mode	Register	Addressing Mode	Mode	Register
Dn	000	register number	d(An, Xi)	110	register number
An*	001	register number	Abs.W	111	000
(An)	010	register number	Abs.L	111	001
(An)+	011	register number	d(PC)	—	—
–(An)	100	register number	d(PC, Xi)	—	—
d(An)	101	register number	Imm	—	—

*Word and Long only.

SUBX

Subtract with Extend

SUBX

Operation: (Destination) − (Source) − X → Destination

Assembler
Syntax:
SUBX Dy, Dx
SUBX −(Ay), −(Ax)

Attributes: Size = (Byte, Word, Long)

Description: Subtract the source operand from the destination operand along with the extend bit and store the result in the destination location. The operands may be addressed in two different ways:

1. Data register to data register: The operands are contained in data registers specified in the instruction.
2. Memory to memory. The operands are contained in memory and addressed with the predecrement addressing mode using the address registers specified in the instruction.

The size of the operation may be specified to be byte, word, or long.

Condition Codes:

X	N	Z	V	C
*	*	*	*	*

N   Set if the result is negative. Cleared otherwise.
Z   Cleared if the result is non-zero. Unchanged otherwise.
V   Set if an overflow is generated. Cleared otherwise.
C   Set if a carry is generated. Cleared otherwise.
X   Set the same as the carry bit.

NOTE

Normally the Z condition code bit is set via programming before the start of an operation. This allows successful tests for zero results upon completion of multiple-precision operations.

Instruction Format:

15	14	13	12	11 10 9	8	7 6	5	4	3	2 1 0
1	0	0	1	Register Rx	1	Size	0	0	R/M	Register Ry

— Continued —

SUBX

Subtract with Extend

SUBX

Instruction Fields:

Register Rx field — Specifies the destination register:
If R/M = 0, specifies a data register.
If R/M = 1, specifies an address register for the predecrement addressing mode.

Size field — Specifies the size of the operation:
00 — byte operation.
01 — word operation.
10 — long operation.

R/M field — Specifies the operand addressing mode:
0 — The operation is data register to data register.
1 — The operation is memory to memory.

Register Ry field — Specifies the source register:
If R/M = 0, specifies a data register.
If R/M = 1, specifies an address register for the predecrement addressing mode.

SWAP   Swap Register Halves   SWAP

Operation: Register [31:16] ↔ Register [15:0]

**Assembler
Syntax:**   SWAP Dn

Attributes: Size = (Word)

Description: Exchange the 16-bit halves of a data register.

Condition Codes:

X	N	Z	V	C
—	*	*	0	0

N   Set if the most significant bit of the 32-bit result is set. Cleared
    otherwise.
Z   Set if the 32-bit result is zero. Cleared otherwise.
V   Always cleared.
C   Always cleared.
X   Not affected.

Instruction Format:

15	14	13	12	11	10	9	8	7	6	5	4	3	2	1	0
0	1	0	0	1	0	0	0	0	1	0	0	0	Register		

Instruction Fields:

Register field — Specifies the data register to swap.

TAS   Test and Set an Operand   TAS

Operation: (Destination) Tested → CC; 1 → bit 7 OF Destination

Assembler Syntax: TAS <ea>

Attributes: Size = (Byte)

Description: Test and set the byte operand addressed by the effective address field. The current value of the operand is tested and N and Z are set accordingly. The high order bit of the operand is set. The operation is indivisible (using a read-modify-write memory cycle) to allow synchronization of several processors.

Condition Codes:

X	N	Z	V	C
—	*	*	0	0

N   Set if the most significant bit of the operand was set. Cleared otherwise.
Z   Set if the operand was zero. Cleared otherwise.
V   Always cleared.
C   Always cleared.
X   Not affected.

Instruction Format:

15	14	13	12	11	10	9	8	7	6	5 4 3	2 1 0
0	1	0	0	1	0	1	0	1	1	Effective Address Mode	Register

Instruction Fields:

Effective Address field — Specifies the location of the tested operand. Only data alterable addressing modes are allowed as shown:

Addressing Mode	Mode	Register	Addressing Mode	Mode	Register
Dn	000	register number	d(An, Xi)	110	register number
An	—	—	Abs.W	111	000
(An)	010	register number	Abs.L	111	001
(An)+	011	register number	d(PC)	—	—
−(An)	100	register number	d(PC, Xi)	—	—
d(An)	101	register number	Imm	—	—

Note: Bus error retry is inhibited on the read portion of the TAS read-modify-write bus cycle to ensure system integrity. The bus error exception is always taken.

TRAP   Trap   TRAP

Operation: PC→ – (SSP); SR→ – (SSP); (Vector)→ PC

Assembler
Syntax: TRAP #<vector>

Attributes: Unsized

Description: The processor initiates exception processing. The vector number is generated to reference the TRAP instruction exception vector specified by the low order four bits of the instruction. Sixteen TRAP instruction vectors are available.

Condition Codes: Not affected.

Instruction Format:

15	14	13	12	11	10	9	8	7	6	5	4	3	2	1	0
0	1	0	0	1	1	1	0	0	1	0	0	Vector			

Instruction Fields:

Vector field — Specifies which trap vector contains the new program counter to be loaded.

TRAPV

Trap on Overflow

TRAPV

Operation: If V then TRAP

**Assembler
Syntax:** TRAPV

Attributes: Unsized

Description: If the overflow condition is on, the processor initiates exception processing. The vector number is generated to reference the TRAPV exception vector. If the overflow condition is off, no operation is performed and execution continues with the next instruction in sequence.

Condition Codes: Not affected.

Instruction Format:

15	14	13	12	11	10	9	8	7	6	5	4	3	2	1	0
0	1	0	0	1	1	1	0	0	1	1	1	0	1	1	0

TST

Test an Operand

TST

Operation: (Destination) Tested → CC

Assembler
Syntax: TST <ea>

Attributes: Size = (Byte, Word, Long)

Description: Compare the operand with zero. No results are saved; however, the condition codes are set according to results of the test. The size of the operation may be specified to be byte, word, or long.

Condition Codes:

```
X  N  Z  V  C
```
—	*	*	0	0

N   Set if the operand is negative. Cleared otherwise.
Z   Set if the operand is zero. Cleared otherwise.
V   Always cleared.
C   Always cleared.
X   Not affected.

Instruction Format:

15	14	13	12	11	10	9	8	7	6	5	4	3	2	1	0
0	1	0	0	1	0	1	0	Size		Effective Address Mode | Register					

Instruction Fields:

Size field — Specifies the size of the operation:
00 — byte operation.
01 — word operation.
10 — long operation.

Effective Address field — Specifies the destination operand. Only data alterable addressing modes are allowed as shown:

Addressing Mode	Mode	Register	Addressing Mode	Mode	Register
Dn	000	register number	d(An, Xi)	110	register number
An	—	—	Abs.W	111	000
(An)	010	register number	Abs.L	111	001
(An)+	011	register number	d(PC)	—	—
−(An)	100	register number	d(PC, Xi)	—	—
d(An)	101	register number	Imm	—	—

UNLK

UNLK   Unlink   **UNLK**

Operation: An → SP; (SP) + → An

Assembler
Syntax: UNLK An

Attributes: Unsized

Description: The stack pointer is loaded from the specified address register. The address register is then loaded with the long word pulled from the top of the stack.

Condition Codes: Not affected.

Instruction Format:

15	14	13	12	11	10	9	8	7	6	5	4	3	2	1	0
0	1	0	0	1	1	1	0	0	1	0	1	1	Register		

Instruction Fields:

Register field — specifies the address register through which the unlinking is to be done.

APPENDIX C
INSTRUCTION FORMAT SUMMARY

C.1 INTRODUCTION

This appendix provides a summary of the first word in each instruction of the instruction set. Table C-1 is an operation code (op-code) map which illustrates how bits 15 through 12 are used to specify the operations. The remaining paragraph groups the instructions according to the op-code map.

Table C-1. Operation Code Map

Bits 15 through 12	Operation	Bits 15 through 12	Operation
0000	Bit Manipulation/MOVEP/Immediate	1000	OR/DIV/SBCD
0001	Move Byte	1001	SUB/SUBX
0010	Move Long	1010	(Unassigned)
0011	Move Word	1011	CMP/EOR
0100	Miscellaneous	1100	AND/MUL/ABCD/EXG
0101	ADDQ/SUBQ/Scc/DBcc	1101	ADD/ADDX
0110	Bcc/BSR	1110	Shift/Rotate
0111	MOVEQ	1111	(Unassigned)

Table C-2. Effective Address Encoding Summary

Addressing Mode	Mode	Register
Data Register Direct	000	register number
Address Register Direct	001	register number
Address Register Indirect	010	register number
Address Register Indirect with Postincrement	011	register number
Address Register Indirect with Predecrement	100	register number
Address Register Indirect with Displacement	101	register number
Address Register Indirect with Index	110	register number
Absolute Short	111	000
Absolute Long	111	001
Program Counter with Displacement	111	010
Program Counter with Index	111	011
Immediate or Status Register	111	100

Table C-3. Conditional Tests

Mnemonic	Condition	Encoding	Test
T	true	0000	1
F	false	0001	0
HI	high	0010	$\overline{C} \cdot \overline{Z}$
LS	low or same	0011	$C + Z$
CC(HS)	carry clear	0100	$\overline{C}$
CS(LO)	carry set	0101	C
NE	not equal	0110	$\overline{Z}$
EQ	equal	0111	Z
VC	overflow clear	1000	$\overline{V}$
VS	overflow set	1001	V
PL	plus	1010	$\overline{N}$
MI	minus	1011	N
GE	greater or equal	1100	$N \cdot V + \overline{N} \cdot \overline{V}$
LT	less than	1101	$N \cdot \overline{V} + \overline{N} \cdot V$
GT	greater than	1110	$N \cdot V \cdot \overline{Z} + \overline{N} \cdot \overline{V} \cdot \overline{Z}$
LE	less or equal	1111	$Z + N \cdot \overline{V} + \overline{N} \cdot V$

OR Immediate

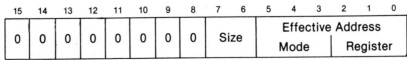

15	14	13	12	11	10	9	8	7	6	5	4	3	2	1	0
0	0	0	0	0	0	0	0	Size		Effective Address Mode			Register		

Size field: 00 = byte
01 = word
10 = long

OR Immediate to CCR

15	14	13	12	11	10	9	8	7	6	5	4	3	2	1	0
0	0	0	0	0	0	0	0	0	0	1	1	1	1	0	0

OR Immediate to SR

15	14	13	12	11	10	9	8	7	6	5	4	3	2	1	0
0	0	0	0	0	0	0	0	0	1	1	1	1	1	0	0

Dynamic Bit

15	14	13	12	11	10	9	8	7	6	5	4	3	2	1	0
0	0	0	0	Data Register			1	Type		Effective Address					
										Mode			Register		

Type field: 00 = TST
01 = CHG
10 = CLR
11 = SET

MOVEP

15	14	13	12	11	10	9	8	7	6	5	4	3	2	1	0
0	0	0	0	Data Register			Op-Mode			0	0	1	Address Register		

Op-Mode field: 100 = transfer word from memory to register
101 = transfer long from memory to register
110 = transfer word from register to memory
111 = transfer long from register to memory

AND Immediate

15	14	13	12	11	10	9	8	7	6	5	4	3	2	1	0
0	0	0	0	0	0	1	0	Size		Effective Address					
										Mode			Register		

Size field: 00 = byte
01 = word
10 = long

AND Immediate to CCR

15	14	13	12	11	10	9	8	7	6	5	4	3	2	1	0
0	0	0	0	0	0	1	0	0	0	1	1	1	1	0	0

AND Immediate to SR

15	14	13	12	11	10	9	8	7	6	5	4	3	2	1	0
0	0	0	0	0	0	1	0	0	1	1	1	1	1	0	0

SUB Immediate

15	14	13	12	11	10	9	8	7	6	5	4	3	2	1	0
0	0	0	0	0	1	0	0	Size		Effective Address					
										Mode			Register		

Size field: 00 = byte
01 = word
10 = long

ADD Immediate

15	14	13	12	11	10	9	8	7	6	5	4	3	2	1	0
0	0	0	0	0	1	1	0	Size		Effective Address					
										Mode			Register		

Size field: 00 = byte
01 = word
10 = long

Static Bit

15	14	13	12	11	10	9	8	7	6	5	4	3	2	1	0
0	0	0	0	1	0	0	0	Type		Effective Address					
										Mode			Register		

Type field: 00 = TST
01 = CHG
10 = CLR
11 = SET

EOR Immediate

15	14	13	12	11	10	9	8	7	6	5	4	3	2	1	0
0	0	0	0	1	0	1	0	Size		Effective Address					
										Mode			Register		

Size field: 00 = byte
01 = word
10 = long

EOR Immediate to CCR

15	14	13	12	11	10	9	8	7	6	5	4	3	2	1	0
0	0	0	0	1	0	1	0	0	0	1	1	1	1	0	0

EOR Immediate to SR

15	14	13	12	11	10	9	8	7	6	5	4	3	2	1	0
0	0	0	0	1	0	1	0	0	1	1	1	1	1	0	0

CMP Immediate

15	14	13	12	11	10	9	8	7	6	5	4	3	2	1	0
0	0	0	0	1	1	0	0	Size		Effective Address					
										Mode			Register		

Size field: 00 = byte
01 = word
10 = word

MOVES   MC68010

15	14	13	12	11	10	9	8	7	6	5	4	3	2	1	0
0	0	0	1	1	1	1	0	Size		Effective Address					
										Mode			Register		

Size field: 00 = byte
01 = word
10 = long

MOVE Byte

15	14	13	12	11	10	9	8	7	6	5	4	3	2	1	0
0	0	0	1	Destination						Source					
				Register			Mode			Mode			Register		

Note register and mode locations

MOVEA Long

14	14	13	12	11 10 9	8	7	6	5 4 3	2 1 0
								Source	
0	0	1	0	Destination Register	0	0	1	Mode	Register

MOVE Long

15	14	13	12	11 10 9	8 7 6	5 4 3	2 1 0
				Destination		Source	
0	0	1	0	Register	Mode	Mode	Register

Note register and mode locations

MOVEA Word

15	14	13	12	11 10 9	8	7	6	5 4 3	2 1 0
								Source	
0	0	1	1	Destination Register	0	0	1	Mode	Register

MOVE Word

15	14	13	12	11 10 9	8 7 6	5 4 3	2 1 0
				Destination		Source	
0	0	1	1	Register	Mode	Mode	Register

Note register and mode locations

NEGX

15	14	13	12	11	10	9	8	7	6	5	4	3	2	1	0
0	1	0	0	0	0	0	0	Size		Effective Address					
										Mode			Register		

Size field: 00 = byte
01 = word
10 = long

MOVE from SR

15	14	13	12	11	10	9	8	7	6	5	4	3	2	1	0
0	1	0	0	0	0	0	0	1	1	Effective Address					
										Mode			Register		

CHK

15	14	13	12	11	10	9	8	7	6	5	4	3	2	1	0
0	1	0	0	Data Register			1	1	0	Effective Address					
										Mode			Register		

LEA

15	14	13	12	11	10	9	8	7	6	5	4	3	2	1	0
0	1	0	0	Address Register			1	1	1	Effective Address					
										Mode			Register		

CLR

15	14	13	12	11	10	9	8	7	6	5	4	3	2	1	0
0	1	0	0	0	0	1	0	Size		Effective Address					
										Mode			Register		

Size field: 00 = byte
01 = word
10 = long

MOVE from CCR   MC68010

15	14	13	12	11	10	9	8	7	6	5	4	3	2	1	0
0	1	0	0	0	0	1	0	1	1	— Effective Address Mode / Register					

Effective Address: Mode | Register

NEG

15	14	13	12	11	10	9	8	7	6	5	4	3	2	1	0
0	1	0	0	0	1	0	0	Size		Effective Address Mode / Register					

Effective Address: Mode | Register

Size field: 00 = byte
01 = word
10 = long

MOVE to CCR

15	14	13	12	11	10	9	8	7	6	5	4	3	2	1	0
0	1	0	0	0	1	0	0	1	1	Effective Address Mode / Register					

Effective Address: Mode | Register

NOT

15	14	13	12	11	10	9	8	7	6	5	4	3	2	1	0
0	1	0	0	0	1	1	0	Size		Effective Address Mode / Register					

Effective Address: Mode | Register

Size field: 00 = byte
01 = word
10 = long

MOVE to SR

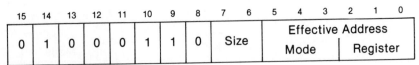

15	14	13	12	11	10	9	8	7	6	5	4	3	2	1	0
0	1	0	0	0	1	1	0	1	1	Effective Address Mode / Register					

Effective Address: Mode | Register

NBCD

15	14	13	12	11	10	9	8	7	6	5	4	3	2	1	0
0	1	0	0	1	0	0	0	0	0	Effective Address Mode			Register		

SWAP

15	14	13	12	11	10	9	8	7	6	5	4	3	2	1	0
0	1	0	0	1	0	0	0	0	1	0	0	0	Data Register		

PEA

15	14	13	12	11	10	9	8	7	6	5	4	3	2	1	0
0	1	0	0	1	0	0	0	0	1	Effective Address Mode			Register		

EXT Word

15	14	13	12	11	10	9	8	7	6	5	4	3	2	1	0
0	1	0	0	1	0	0	0	1	0	0	0	0	Data Register		

MOVEM Registers to EA

15	14	13	12	11	10	9	8	7	6	5	4	3	2	1	0
0	1	0	0	1	0	0	0	1	Sz	Effective Address Mode			Register		

Sz field: 0 = word transfer
1 = long transfer

EXT Long

15	14	13	12	11	10	9	8	7	6	5	4	3	2	1	0
0	1	0	0	1	0	0	0	1	1	0	0	0	Data Register		

TST

15	14	13	12	11	10	9	8	7	6	5	4	3	2	1	0
0	1	0	0	1	0	1	0	Size		Effective Address Mode			Register		

Size field: 00 = byte
01 = word
10 = long

TAS

15	14	13	12	11	10	9	8	7	6	5	4	3	2	1	0
0	1	0	0	1	0	1	0	1	1	Effective Address Mode			Register		

ILLEGAL

15	14	13	12	11	10	9	8	7	6	5	4	3	2	1	0
0	1	0	0	1	0	1	0	1	1	1	1	1	1	0	0

MOVEM EA to Registers

15	14	13	12	11	10	9	8	7	6	5	4	3	2	1	0
0	1	0	0	1	1	0	0	1	Sz	Effective Address Mode			Register		

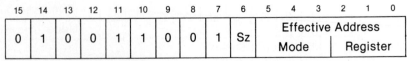

Sz field: 0 = word transfer
1 = long transfer

TRAP

15	14	13	12	11	10	9	8	7	6	5	4	3	2	1	0
0	1	0	0	1	1	1	0	0	1	0	0	Vector			

LINK

15	14	13	12	11	10	9	8	7	6	5	4	3	2	1	0
0	1	0	0	1	1	1	0	0	1	0	1	0	Address Register		

UNLK

15	14	13	12	11	10	9	8	7	6	5	4	3	2	1	0
0	1	0	0	1	1	1	0	0	1	0	1	1	Address Register		

MOVE to USP

15	14	13	12	11	10	9	8	7	6	5	4	3	2	1	0
0	1	0	0	1	1	1	0	0	1	1	0	0	Address Register		

MOVE from USP

15	14	13	12	11	10	9	8	7	6	5	4	3	2	1	0
0	1	0	0	1	1	1	0	0	1	1	0	1	Address Register		

RESET

15	14	13	12	11	10	9	8	7	6	5	4	3	2	1	0
0	1	0	0	1	1	1	0	0	1	1	1	0	0	0	0

NOP

15	14	13	12	11	10	9	8	7	6	5	4	3	2	1	0
0	1	0	0	1	1	1	0	0	1	1	1	0	0	0	1

STOP

15	14	13	12	11	10	9	8	7	6	5	4	3	2	1	0
0	1	0	0	1	1	1	0	0	1	1	1	0	0	1	0

RTE

15	14	13	12	11	10	9	8	7	6	5	4	3	2	1	0
0	1	0	0	1	1	1	0	0	1	1	1	0	0	1	1

RTD   MC68010

15	14	13	12	11	10	9	8	7	6	5	4	3	2	1	0
0	1	0	0	1	1	1	0	0	1	1	1	0	1	0	0

RTS

15	14	13	12	11	10	9	8	7	6	5	4	3	2	1	0
0	1	0	0	1	1	1	0	0	1	1	1	0	1	0	1

TRAPV

15	14	13	12	11	10	9	8	7	6	5	4	3	2	1	0
0	1	0	0	1	1	1	0	0	1	1	1	0	1	1	0

RTR

15	14	13	12	11	10	9	8	7	6	5	4	3	2	1	0
0	1	0	0	1	1	1	0	0	1	1	1	0	1	1	1

MOVEC   **MC68010**

15	14	13	12	11	10	9	8	7	6	5	4	3	2	1	0
0	1	0	0	1	1	1	0	0	1	1	1	1	0	1	dr

dr field: 0 = control register to general register
1 = general register to control register

JSR

15	14	13	12	11	10	9	8	7	6	5	4	3	2	1	0
0	1	0	0	1	1	1	0	1	0	Effective Address					
										Mode			Register		

JMP

15	14	13	12	11	10	9	8	7	6	5	4	3	2	1	0
0	1	0	0	1	1	1	0	1	1	Effective Mode					
										Mode			Register		

ADDQ

15	14	13	12	11	10	9	8	7	6	5	4	3	2	1	0
0	1	0	1	Data			0	Size		Effective Address Mode			Register		

Data field: Three bits of immediate data, 0, 1-7 representing a range of
8, 1 to 7 respectively.

Size field: 00 = byte
01 = word
10 = long

Scc

15	14	13	12	11	10	9	8	7	6	5	4	3	2	1	0
0	1	0	1	Condition				1	1	Effective Address Mode			Register		

Condition field:
0000 = true   1000 = overflow clear
0001 = false   1001 = overflow set
0010 = high   1010 = plus
0011 = low or same   1011 = minus
0100 = carry clear   1100 = greater or equal
0101 = carry set   1101 = less than
0110 = not equal   1110 = greater than
0111 = equal   1111 = less or equal

DBcc

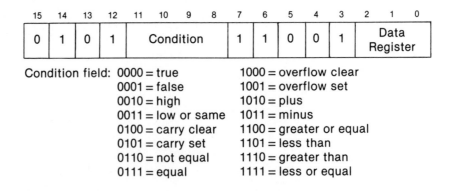

15	14	13	12	11	10	9	8	7	6	5	4	3	2	1	0
0	1	0	1	Condition				1	1	0	0	1	Data Register		

Condition field:
0000 = true   1000 = overflow clear
0001 = false   1001 = overflow set
0010 = high   1010 = plus
0011 = low or same   1011 = minus
0100 = carry clear   1100 = greater or equal
0101 = carry set   1101 = less than
0110 = not equal   1110 = greater than
0111 = equal   1111 = less or equal

SUBQ

15	14	13	12	11	10	9	8	7	6	5	4	3	2	1	0
0	1	0	1	Data			1	Size		Effective Address					
										Mode			Register		

Data field: Three bits of immediate data, 0, 1-7 representing a range of
8, 1 to 7 respectively.
Size field: 00 = byte
01 = word
10 = long

Bcc

15	14	13	12	11	10	9	8	7	6	5	4	3	2	1	0
0	1	1	0	Condition				8-Bit Displacement							

Condition field: 0010 = high   1001 = overflow set
                0011 = low or same   1010 = plus
                0100 = carry clear   1011 = minus
                0101 = carry set   1100 = greater or equal
                0110 = not equal   1101 = less than
                0111 = equal   1110 = greater than
                1000 = overflow clear 1111 = less or equal

BRA

15	14	13	12	11	10	9	8	7	6	5	4	3	2	1	0
0	1	1	0	0	0	0	0	8-Bit Displacement							

BSR

15	14	13	12	11	10	9	8	7	6	5	4	3	2	1	0
0	1	1	0	0	0	0	1	8-Bit Displacement							

MOVEQ

15	14	13	12	11	10	9	8	7	6	5	4	3	2	1	0
0	1	1	1	Data Register			0	Data							

Data field: Data is sign extended to a long operand and all 32 bits are transferred to the data register.

OR

15	14	13	12	11	10	9	8	7	6	5	4	3	2	1	0
1	0	0	0	Data Register			Op-Mode			Effective Address Mode			Register		

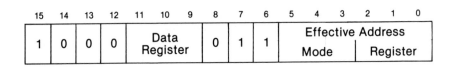

Op-Mode field:

Byte	Word	Long	Operation
000	001	010	$(<Dn>)v(<ea>)\rightarrow Dn$
100	101	110	$(<ea>)v(<Dn>)\rightarrow ea$

DIVU

15	14	13	12	11	10	9	8	7	6	5	4	3	2	1	0
1	0	0	0	Data Register			0	1	1	Effective Address Mode			Register		

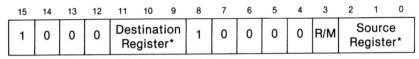

SBCD

15	14	13	12	11	10	9	8	7	6	5	4	3	2	1	0
1	0	0	0	Destination Register*			1	0	0	0	0	R/M	Source Register*		

R/M field: 0 = data register to data register
　　　　　　 1 = memory to memory
*If R/M = 0, specifies a data register.
　If R/M = 1, specifies an address register for the predecrement addressing mode.

DIVS

15	14	13	12	11 10 9	8	7	6	5 4 3	2 1 0
								Effective Address	
1	0	0	0	Data Register	1	1	1	Mode	Register

SUB

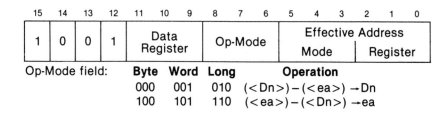

15	14	13	12	11 10 9	8 7 6	5 4 3	2 1 0
						Effective Address	
1	0	0	1	Data Register	Op-Mode	Mode	Register

Op-Mode field:

Byte	Word	Long	Operation
000	001	010	(\<Dn>) – (\<ea>) →Dn
100	101	110	(\<ea>) – (\<Dn>) →ea

SUBA

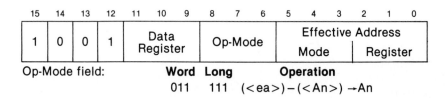

15	14	13	12	11 10 9	8 7 6	5 4 3	2 1 0
						Effective Address	
1	0	0	1	Data Register	Op-Mode	Mode	Register

Op-Mode field:

Word	Long	Operation
011	111	(\<ea>) – (\<An>) →An

SUBX

15	14	13	12	11 10 9	8	7 6	5	4	3	2 1 0
1	0	0	1	Destination Register*	1	Size	0	0	R/M	Source Register*

Size field: 00 = byte
                01 = word
                10 = long
R/M field: 0 = data register to data register
               1 = memory to memory
*If R/M = 0, specifies a data register.
 If R/M = 1, specifies an address register for the predecrement addressing
          mode.

CMP

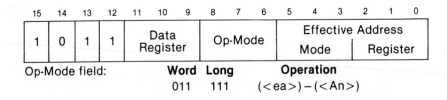

15	14	13	12	11 10 9	8 7 6	5 4 3	2 1 0
						Effective Address	
1	0	1	1	Data Register	Op-Mode	Mode	Register

Op-Mode field:

	Byte	**Word**	**Long**	**Operation**
	000	001	010	$(<Dn>) - (<ea>)$

CMPA

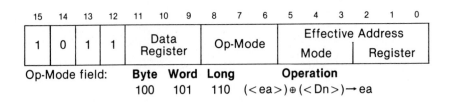

15	14	13	12	11 10 9	8 7 6	5 4 3	2 1 0
						Effective Address	
1	0	1	1	Data Register	Op-Mode	Mode	Register

Op-Mode field:

	Word	**Long**	**Operation**
	011	111	$(<ea>) - (<An>)$

EOR

15	14	13	12	11 10 9	8 7 6	5 4 3	2 1 0
						Effective Address	
1	0	1	1	Data Register	Op-Mode	Mode	Register

Op-Mode field:

	Byte	**Word**	**Long**	**Operation**
	100	101	110	$(<ea>) \oplus (<Dn>) \rightarrow ea$

CMPM

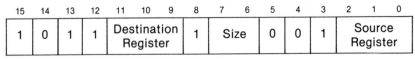

15	14	13	12	11 10 9	8	7 6	5	4	3	2 1 0
1	0	1	1	Destination Register	1	Size	0	0	1	Source Register

Size field: 00 = byte
01 = word
10 = long

AND

15	14	13	12	11	10	9	8	7	6	5	4	3	2	1	0
1	1	0	0	Data Register			Op-Mode			Effective Address					
										Mode			Register		

Op-Mode field:

	Byte	Word	Long	Operation
	000	001	010	$(<Dn>)\Lambda(<ea>) \rightarrow Dn$
	100	101	110	$(<ea>)\Lambda(<Dn>) \rightarrow ea$

MULU

15	14	13	12	11	10	9	8	7	6	5	4	3	2	1	0
1	1	0	0	Data Register			0	1	1	Effective Address					
										Mode			Register		

ABCD

15	14	13	12	11	10	9	8	7	6	5	4	3	2	1	0
1	1	0	0	Destination Register*			1	0	0	0	0	R/M	Source Register*		

R/M field: 0 = data register to data register
1 = memory to memory
*If R/M = 0, specifies a data register.
If R/M = 1, specifies an address register for the predecrement addressing
mode.

EXG Data Registers

15	14	13	12	11	10	9	8	7	6	5	4	3	2	1	0
1	1	0	0	Data Register			1	0	1	0	0	0	Data Register		

EXG Address Registers

15	14	13	12	11	10	9	8	7	6	5	4	3	2	1	0
1	1	0	0	Address Register			1	0	1	0	0	1	Address Register		

EXG Data Register and Address Register

15	14	13	12	11	10	9	8	7	6	5	4	3	2	1	0
1	1	0	0	Data Register			1	1	0	0	0	1	Address Register		

MULS

15	14	13	12	11	10	9	8	7	6	5	4	3	2	1	0
1	1	0	0	Data Register			1	1	1	Effective Address Mode			Register		

ADD

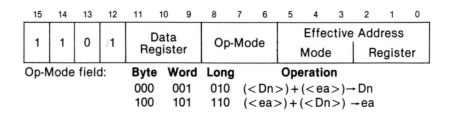

15	14	13	12	11	10	9	8	7	6	5	4	3	2	1	0
1	1	0	/1	Data Register			Op-Mode			Effective Address Mode			Register		

Op-Mode field:

Byte	Word	Long	Operation
000	001	010	$(<Dn>) + (<ea>) \rightarrow Dn$
100	101	110	$(<ea>) + (<Dn>) \rightarrow ea$

ADDA

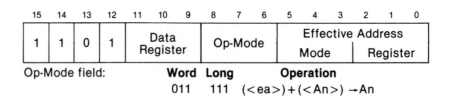

15	14	13	12	11	10	9	8	7	6	5	4	3	2	1	0
1	1	0	1	Data Register			Op-Mode			Effective Address Mode			Register		

Op-Mode field:

Word	Long	Operation
011	111	$(<ea>) + (<An>) \rightarrow An$

ADDX

15	14	13	12	11	10	9	8	7	6	5	4	3	2	1	0
1	1	0	1	Destination Register*			1	Size		0	0	R/M	Source Register*		

Size field: 00 = byte
    01 = word
    10 = long
R/M field: 0 = data register to data register
    1 = memory to memory
*If R/M = 0, specifies a data register.
 If R/M = 1, specifies an address register for the predecrement addressing
   mode.

SHIFT/ROTATE — Register

15	14	13	12	11	10	9	8	7	6	5	4	3	2	1	0
1	1	1	0	Count/ Register			dr	Size		i/r	Type		Data Register		

Count/Register field: If i/r field = 0, specifies shift count
       If i/r field = 1, specifies a data register that contains the
        shift count
dr field: 0 = right
   1 = left
Size field: 00 = byte
    01 = word
    10 = long
i/r field: 0 = immediate shift count
   1 = register shift count
Type field: 00 = arithmetic shift
    01 = logical shift
    10 = rotate with extend
    11 = rotate

SHIFT/ROTATE — Memory

15	14	13	12	11	10	9	8	7	6	5	4	3	2	1	0
1	1	1	0	0	Type		dr	1	1	Effective Address					
										Mode			Register		

Type field: 00 = arithmetic shift
    01 = logical shift
    10 = rotate with extend
    11 = rotate
dr field: 0 = right
   1 = left

185

APPENDIX D
MC68000 INSTRUCTION EXECUTION TIMES

D.1 INTRODUCTION

This Appendix contains listings of the instruction execution times in terms of external clock (CLK) periods. In this data, it is assumed that both memory read and write cycle times are four clock periods. A longer memory cycle will cause the generation of wait states which must be added to the total instruction time.

The number of bus read and write cycles for each instruction is also included with the timing data. This data is enclosed in parenthesis following the number of clock periods and is shown as: (r/w) where r is the number of read cycles and w is the number of write cycles included in the clock period number. Recalling that either a read or write cycle requires four clock periods, a timing number given as 18(3/1) relates to 12 clock periods for the three read cycles, plus 4 clock periods for the one write cycle, plus 2 cycles required for some internal function of the processor.

NOTE
The number of periods includes instruction fetch and all applicable operand fetches and stores.

D.2 OPERAND EFFECTIVE ADDRESS CALCULATION TIMING

Table D-1 lists the number of clock periods required to compute an instruction's effective address. It includes fetching of any extension words, the address computation, and fetching of the memory operand. The number of bus read and write cycles is shown in parenthesis as (r/w). Note there are no write cycles involved in processing the effective address.

Table D-1. Effective Address Calculation Times

Addressing Mode		Byte, Word	Long
	Register		
Dn	Data Register Direct	0(0/0)	0(0/0)
An	Address Register Direct	0(0/0)	0(0/0)
	Memory		
(An)	Address Register Indirect	4(1/0)	8(2/0)
(An) +	Address Register Indirect with Postincrement	4(1/0)	8(2/0)
− (An)	Address Register Indirect with Predecrement	6(1/0)	10(2/0)
d(An)	Address Register Indirect with Displacement	8(2/0)	12(3/0)
d(An, ix)*	Address Register Indirect with Index	10(2/0)	14(3/0)
xxx.W	Absolute Short	8(2/0)	12(3/0)
xxx.L	Absolute Long	12(3/0)	16(4/0)
d(PC)	Program Counter with Displacement	8(2/0)	12(3/0)
d(PC, ix)*	Program Counter with Index	10(2/0)	14(3/0)
#xxx	Immediate	4(1/0)	8(2/0)

*The size of the index register (ix) does not affect execution time.

D.3 MOVE INSTRUCTION EXECUTION TIMES

Tables D-2 and D-3 indicate the number of clock periods for the move instruction. This data includes instruction fetch, operand reads, and operand writes. The number of bus read and write cycles is shown in parenthesis as (r/w).

Table D-2. Move Byte and Word Instruction Execution Times

Source	Destination								
	Dn	An	(An)	(An)+	-(An)	d(An)	d(An, ix)*	xxx.W	xxx.L
Dn	4(1/0)	4(1/0)	8(1/1)	8(1/1)	8(1/1)	12(2/1)	14(2/1)	12(2/1)	16(3/1)
An	4(1/0)	4(1/0)	8(1/1)	8(1/1)	8(1/1)	12(2/1)	14(2/1)	12(2/1)	16(3/1)
(An)	8(2/0)	8(2/0)	12(2/1)	12(2/1)	12(2/1)	16(3/1)	18(3/1)	16(3/1)	20(4/1)
(An)+	8(2/0)	8(2/0)	12(2/1)	12(2/1)	12(2/1)	16(3/1)	18(3/1)	16(3/1)	20(4/1)
-(An)	10(2/0)	10(2/0)	14(2/1)	14(2/1)	14(2/1)	18(3/1)	20(3/1)	18(3/1)	22(4/1)
d(An)	12(3/0)	12(3/0)	16(3/1)	16(3/1)	16(3/1)	20(4/1)	22(4/1)	20(4/1)	24(5/1)
d(An, ix)*	14(3/0)	14(3/0)	18(3/1)	18(3/1)	18(3/1)	22(4/1)	24(4/1)	22(4/1)	26(5/1)
xxx.W	12(3/0)	12(3/0)	16(3/1)	16(3/1)	16(3/1)	20(4/1)	22(4/1)	20(4/1)	24(5/1)
xxx.L	16(4/0)	16(4/0)	20(4/1)	20(4/1)	20(4/1)	24(5/1)	26(5/1)	24(5/1)	28(6/1)
d(PC)	12(3/0)	12(3/0)	16(3/1)	16(3/1)	16(3/1)	20(4/1)	22(4/1)	20(4/1)	24(5/1)
d(PC, ix)*	14(3/0)	14(3/0)	18(3/1)	18(3/1)	18(3/1)	22(4/1)	24(4/1)	22(4/1)	26(5/1)
#xxx	8(2/0)	8(2/0)	12(2/1)	12(2/1)	12(2/1)	16(3/1)	18(3/1)	16(3/1)	20(4/1)

*The size of the index register (ix) does not affect execution time.

Table D-3. Move Long Instruction Execution Times

Source	Destination								
	Dn	An	(An)	(An)+	-(An)	d(An)	d(An, ix)*	xxx.W	xxx.L
Dn	4(1/0)	4(1/0)	12(1/2)	12(1/2)	12(1/2)	16(2/2)	18(2/2)	16(2/2)	20(3/2)
An	4(1/0)	4(1/0)	12(1/2)	12(1/2)	12(1/2)	16(2/2)	18(2/2)	16(2/2)	20(3/2)
(An)	12(3/0)	12(3/0)	20(3/2)	20(3/2)	20(3/2)	24(4/2)	26(4/2)	24(4/2)	28(5/2)
(An)+	12(3/0)	12(3/0)	20(3/2)	20(3/2)	20(3/2)	24(4/2)	26(4/2)	24(4/2)	28(5/2)
-(An)	14(3/0)	14(3/0)	22(3/2)	22(3/2)	22(3/2)	26(4/2)	28(4/2)	26(4/2)	30(5/2)
d(An)	16(4/0)	16(4/0)	24(4/2)	24(4/2)	24(4/2)	28(5/2)	30(5/2)	28(5/2)	32(6/2)
d(An, ix)*	18(4/0)	18(4/0)	26(4/2)	26(4/2)	26(4/2)	30(5/2)	32(5/2)	30(5/2)	34(6/2)
xxx.W	16(4/0)	16(4/0)	24(4/2)	24(4/2)	24(4/2)	28(5/2)	30(5/2)	28(5/2)	32(6/2)
xxx.L	20(5/0)	20(5/0)	28(5/2)	28(5/2)	28(5/2)	32(6/2)	34(6/2)	32(6/2)	36(7/2)
d(PC)	16(4/0)	16(4/0)	24(4/2)	24(4/2)	24(4/2)	28(5/2)	30(5/2)	28(5/2)	32(5/2)
d(PC, ix)*	18(4/0)	18(4/0)	26(4/2)	26(4/2)	26(4/2)	30(5/2)	32(5/2)	30(5/2)	34(6/2)
#xxx	12(3/0)	12(3/0)	20(3/2)	20(3/2)	20(3/2)	24(4/2)	26(4/2)	24(4/2)	28(5/2)

*The size of the index register (ix) does not affect execution time.

D.4 STANDARD INSTRUCTION EXECUTION TIMES

The number of clock periods shown in Table D-4 indicates the time required to perform the operations, store the results, and read the next instruction. The number of bus read and write cycles is shown in parenthesis as (r/w). The number of clock periods and the number of read and write cycles must be added respectively to those of the effective address calculation where indicated.

In Table D-4 the headings have the following meanings: An = address register operand, Dn = data register operand, ea = an operand specified by an effective address, and M = memory effective address operand.

Table D-4. Standard Instruction Execution Times

Instruction	Size	op<ea>, An†	op<ea>, Dn	op Dn, <M>
ADD	Byte, Word	8(1/0) +	4(1/0) +	8(1/1) +
	Long	6(1/0) + * *	6(1/0) + * *	12(1/2) +
AND	Byte, Word	—	4(1/0) +	8(1/1) +
	Long	—	6(1/0) + * *	12(1/2) +
CMP	Byte, Word	6(1/0) +	4(1/0) +	—
	Long	6(1/0) +	6(1/0) +	—
DIVS	—	—	158(1/0) + *	—
DIVU	—	—	140(1/0) + *	—
EOR	Byte, Word	—	4(1/0) * * *	8(1/1) +
	Long	—	8(1/0) * * *	12(1/2) +
MULS	—	—	70(1/0) + *	—
MULU	—	—	70(1/0) + *	—
OR	Byte, Word	—	4(1/0) +	8(1/1) +
	Long	—	6(1/0) + * *	12(1/2) +
SUB	Byte, Word	8(1/0) +	4(1/0) +	8(1/1) +
	Long	6(1/0) + * *	6(1/0) + * *	12(1/2) +

NOTES:
+ add effective address calculation time
† word or long only
* indicates maximum value
* * The base time of six clock periods is increased to eight if the effective address mode is register direct or immediate (effective address time should also be added).
* * * Only available effective address mode is data register direct.
DIVS, DIVU — The divide algorithm used by the MC68000 provides less than 10% difference between the best and worst case timings.
MULS, MULU — The multiply algorithm requires $38 + 2n$ clocks where n is defined as:
MULU: n = the number of ones in the <ea>
MULS: n = concatanate the <ea> with a zero as the LSB; n is the resultant number of 10 or 01 patterns in the 17-bit source; i.e., worst case happens when the source is $5555.

D.5 IMMEDIATE INSTRUCTION EXECUTION TIMES

The number of clock periods shown in Table D-5 includes the time to fetch immediate operands, perform the operations, store the results, and read the next operation. The number of bus read and write cycles is shown in parenthesis as (r/w). The number of clock periods and the number of read and write cycles must be added respectively to those of the effective address calculation where indicated.

In Table D-5, the headings have the following meanings: # = immediate operand, Dn = data register operand, An = address register operand, and M = memory operand. SR = status register.

Table D-5. Immediate Instruction Execution Times

Instruction	Size	op #, Dn	op #, An	op #, M
ADDI	Byte, Word	8(2/0)	—	12(2/1) +
	Long	16(3/0)	—	20(3/2) +
ADDQ	Byte, Word	4(1/0)	8(1/0) *	8(1/1) +
	Long	8(1/0)	8(1/0)	12(1/2) +
ANDI	Byte, Word	8(2/0)	—	12(2/1) +
	Long	16(3/0)	—	20(3/1) +
CMPI	Byte, Word	8(2/0)	—	8(2/0) +
	Long	14(3/0)	—	12(3/0) +
EORI	Byte, Word	8(2/0)	—	12(2/1) +
	Long	16(3/0)	—	20(3/2) +
MOVEQ	Long	4(1/0)	—	—
ORI	Byte, Word	8(2/0)	—	12(2/1) +
	Long	16(3/0)	—	20(3/2) +
SUBI	Byte, Word	8(2/0)	—	12(2/1) +
	Long	16(3/0)	—	20(3/2) +
SUBQ	Byte, Word	4(1/0)	8(1/0) *	8(1/1) +
	Long	8(1/0)	8(1/0)	12(1/2) +

+ add effective address calculation time
* word only

D.6 SINGLE OPERAND INSTRUCTION EXECUTION TIMES

Table D-6 indicates the number of clock periods for the single operand instructions. The number of bus read and write cycles is shown in parenthesis as (r/w). The number of clock periods and the number of read and write cycles must be added respectively to those of the effective address calculation where indicated.

Table D-6. Single Operand Instruction Execution Times

Instruction	Size	Register	Memory
CLR	Byte, Word	4(1/0)	8(1/1) +
	Long	6(1/0)	12(1/2) +
NBCD	Byte	6(1/0)	8(1/1) +
NEG	Byte, Word	4(1/0)	8(1/1) +
	Long	6(1/0)	12(1/2) +
NEGX	Byte, Word	4(1/0)	8(1/1) +
	Long	6(1/0)	12(1/2) +
NOT	Byte, Word	4(1/0)	8(1/1) +
	Long	6(1/0)	12(1/2) +
S_{CC}	Byte, False	4(1/0)	8(1/1) +
	Byte, True	6(1/0)	8(1/1) +
TAS	Byte	4(1/0)	10(1/1) +
TST	Byte, Word	4(1/0)	4(1/0) +
	Long	4(1/0)	4(1/0) +

\+ add effective address calculation time

D.7 SHIFT/ROTATE INSTRUCTION EXECUTION TIMES

Table D-7 indicates the number of clock periods for the shift and rotate instructions. The number of bus read and write cycles is shown in parenthesis as (r/w). The number of clock periods and the number of read and write cycles must be added respectively to those of the effective address calculation where indicated.

Table D-7. Shift/Rotate Instruction Execution Times

Instruction	Size	Register	Memory
ASR, ASL	Byte, Word	6 + 2n(1/0)	8(1/1) +
	Long	8 + 2n(1/0)	—
LSR, LSL	Byte, Word	6 + 2n(1/0)	8(1/1) +
	Long	8 + 2n(1/0)	—
ROR, ROL	Byte, Word	6 + 2n(1/0)	8(1/1) +
	Long	8 + 2n(1/0)	—
ROXR, ROXL	Byte, Word	6 + 2n(1/0)	8(1/1) +
	Long	8 + 2n(1/0)	—

\+ add effective address calculation time
n is the shift count

D.8 BIT MANIPULATION INSTRUCTION EXECUTION TIMES

Table D-8 indicates the number of clock periods required for the bit manipulation instructions. The number of bus read and write cycles is shown in parenthesis as (r/w). The number of clock periods and the number of read and write cycles must be added respectively to those of the effective address calculation where indicated.

Table D-8. Bit Manipulation Instruction Execution Times

Instruction	Size	Dynamic		Static	
		Register	Memory	Register	Memory
BCHG	Byte	—	8(1/1) +	—	12(2/1) +
	Long	8(1/0) *	—	12(2/0) *	—
BCLR	Byte	—	8(1/1) +	—	12(2/1) +
	Long	10(1/0) *	—	14(2/0) *	—
BSET	Byte	—	8(1/1) +	—	12(2/1) +
	Long	8(1/0) *	—	12(2/0) *	—
BTST	Byte	—	4(1/0) +	—	8(2/0) +
	Long	6(1/0)	—	10(2/0)	—

+ add effective address calculation time
* indicates maximum value

D.9 CONDITIONAL INSTRUCTION EXECUTION TIMES

Table D-9 indicates the number of clock periods required for the conditional instructions. The number of bus read and write cycles is indicated in parenthesis as (r/w). The number of clock periods and the number of read and write cycles must be added respectively to those of the effective address calculation where indicated.

Table D-9. Conditional Instruction Execution Times

Instruction	Displacement	Branch Taken	Branch Not Taken
B_CC	Byte	10(2/0)	8(1/0)
	Word	10(2/0)	12(2/0)
BRA	Byte	10(2/0)	—
	Word	10(2/0)	—
BSR	Byte	18(2/2)	—
	Word	18(2/2)	—
DB_CC	CC true	—	12(2/0)
	CC false	10(2/0)	14(3/0)

+ add effective address calculation time
* indicates maximum value

192

D.10 JMP, JSR, LEA, PEA, AND MOVEM INSTRUCTION EXECUTION TIMES

Table D-10 indicates the number of clock periods required for the jump, jump-to-subroutine, load effective address, push effective address, and move multiple registers instructions. The number of bus read and write cycles is shown in parenthesis as (r/w).

Table D-10. JMP, JSR, LEA, PEA, and MOVEM Instruction Execution Times

Instr	Size	(An)	(An) +	– (An)	d(An)	d(An, ix) +	xxx.W	xxx.L	d(PC)	d(PC, ix) *
JMP	–	8(2/0)	–	–	10(2/0)	14(3/0)	10(2/0)	12(3/0)	10(2/0)	14(3/0)
JSR	–	16(2/2)	–	–	18(2/2)	22(2/2)	18(2/2)	20(3/2)	18(2/2)	22(2/2)
LEA	–	4(1/0)	–	–	8(2/0)	12(2/0)	8(2/0)	12(3/0)	8(2/0)	12(2/0)
PEA	–	12(1/2)	–	–	16(2/2)	20(2/2)	16(2/2)	20(3/2)	16(2/2)	20(2/2)
MOVEM M → R	Word	12+4n (3+n/0)	12+4n (3+n/0)	–	16+4n (4+n/0)	18+4n (4+n/0)	16+4n (4+n/0)	20+4n (5+n/0)	16+4n (4+n/0)	18+4n (4+n/0)
	Long	12+8n (3+2n/0)	12+8n (3+2n/0)	–	16+8n (4+2n/0)	18+8n (4+2n/0)	16+8n (4+2n/0)	20+8n (5+2n/0)	16+8n (4+2n/0)	18+8n (4+2n/0)
MOVEM R → M	Word	8+4n (2/n)	–	8+4n (2/n)	12+4n (3/n)	14+4n (3/n)	12+4n (3/n)	16+4n (4/n)	–	–
	Long	8+8n (2/2n)	–	8+8n (2/2n)	12+8n (3/2n)	14+8n (3/2n)	12+8n (3/2n)	16+8n (4/2n)	–	–

n is the number of registers to move
* is the size of the index register (ix) does not affect the instruction's execution time

D 11 MULTI-PRECISION INSTRUCTION EXECUTION TIMES

Table D-11 indicates the number of clock periods for the multi-precision instructions. The number of clock periods includes the time to fetch both operands, peform the operations, store the results, and read the next instructions. The number of read and write cycles is shown in parenthesis as (r/w).

In Table D-11, the headings have the following meanings: Dn = data register operand and M = memory operand.

Table D-11. Multi-Precision Instruction Execution Times

Instruction	Size	op Dn, Dn	op M, M
ADDX	Byte, Word	4(1/0)	18(3/1)
	Long	8(1/0)	30(5/2)
CMPM	Byte, Word	–	12(3/0)
	Long	–	20(5/0)
SUBX	Byte, Word	4(1/0)	18(3/1)
	Long	8(1/0)	30(5/2)
ABCD	Byte	6(1/0)	18(3/1)
SBCD	Byte	6(1/0)	18(3/1)

D.12 MISCELLANEOUS INSTRUCTION EXECUTION TIMES

Tables D-12 and D-13 indicate the number of clock periods for the following miscellaneous instructions. The number of bus read and write cycles is shown in parenthesis as (r/w). The number of clock periods plus the number of read and write cycles must be added to those of the effective address calculation where indicated.

Table D-12. Miscellaneous Instruction Execution Times

Instruction	Size	Register	Memory
ANDI to CCR	Byte	20(3/0)	—
ANDI to SR	Word	20(3/0)	—
CHK	—	10(1/0) +	—
EORI to CCR	Byte	20(3/0)	—
EORI to SR	Word	20(3/0)	—
ORI to CCR	Byte	20(3/0)	—
ORI to SR	Word	20(3/0)	—
MOVE from SR	—	6(1/0)	8(1/1) +
MOVE to CCR	—	12(2/0)	12(2/0) +
MOVE to SR	—	12(2/0)	12(2/0) +
EXG	—	6(1/0)	—
EXT	Word	4(1/0)	—
EXT	Long	4(1/0)	—
LINK	—	16(2/2)	—
MOVE from USP	—	4(1/0)	—
MOVE to USP	—	4(1/0)	—
NOP	—	4(1/0)	—
RESET	—	132(1/0)	—
RTE	—	20(5/0)	—
RTR	—	20(5/0)	—
RTS	—	16(4/0)	—
STOP	—	4(0/0)	—
SWAP	—	4(1/0)	—
TRAPV	—	4(1/0)	—
UNLK	—	12(3/0)	—

+ add effective address calculation time

Table D-13. Move Peripheral Instruction Execution Times

Instruction	Size	Register → Memory	Memory → Register
MOVEP	Word	16(2/2)	16(4/0)
MOVEP	Long	24(2/4)	24(6/0)

D.13 EXCEPTION PROCESSING EXECUTION TIMES

Table D-14 indicates the number of clock periods for exception processing. The number of clock periods includes the time for all stacking, the vector fetch, and the fetch of the first two instruction words of the handler routine. The number of bus read and write cycles is shown in parenthesis as (r/w).

Table D-14. Exception Processing Execution Times

Exception	Periods
Address Error	50(4/7)
Bus Error	50(4/7)
CHK Instruction	44(5/4) +
Divide by Zero	42(5/4)
Illegal Instruction	34(4/3)
Interrupt	44(5/3) *
Privilege Violation	34(4/3)
RESET**	40(6/0)
Trace	34(4/3)
TRAP Instruction	38(4/4)
TRAPV Instruction	34(4/3)

+ add effective address calculation time

* The interrupt acknowledge cycle is assumed to take four clock periods.

** Indicates the time from when $\overline{RESET}$ and $\overline{HALT}$ are first sampled as negated to when instruction execution starts.

195

APPENDIX E
MC68008 INSTRUCTION EXECUTION TIMES

E.1 INTRODUCTION

This Appendix contains listings of the instruction execution times in terms of external clock (CLK) periods. In this data, it is assumed that both memory read and write cycle times are four clock periods. A longer memory cycle will cause the generation of wait states which must be added to the total instruction time.

The number of bus read and write cycles for each instruction is also included with the timing data. This data is enclosed in parenthesis following the number of clock periods and is shown as: (r/w) where r is the number of read cycles and w is the number of write cycles included in the clock period number. Recalling that either a read or write cycle requires four clock periods, a timing number given as 18(3/1) relates to 12 clock periods for the three read cycles, plus 4 clock periods for the one write cycle, plus 2 cycles required for some internal function of the processor.

NOTE
The number of periods includes instruction fetch and all applicable operand fetches and stores.

E.2 OPERAND EFFECTIVE ADDRESS CALCULATION TIMES

Table E-1 lists the number of clock periods required to compute an instruction's effective address. It includes fetching of any extension words, the address computation, and fetching of the memory operand. The number of bus read and write cycles is shown in parenthesis as (r/w). Note there are no write cycles involved in processing the effective address.

Table E-1. Effective Address Calculation Times

Addressing Mode		Byte	Word	Long
	Register			
Dn	Data Register Direct	0(0/0)	0(0/0)	0(0/0)
An	Address Register Direct	0(0/0)	0(0/0)	0(0/0)
	Memory			
(An)	Address Register Indirect	4(1/0)	8(2/0)	16(4/0)
(An)+	Address Register Indirect with Postincrement	4(1/0)	8(2/0)	16(4/0)
−(An)	Address Register Indirect with Predecrement	6(1/0)	10(2/0)	18(4/0)
d(An)	Address Register Indirect with Displacement	12(3/0)	16(4/0)	24(6/0)
d(An, ix)*	Address Register Indirect with Index	14(3/0)	18(4/0)	26(6/0)
xxx.W	Absolute Short	12(3/0)	16(4/0)	24(6/0)
xxx.L	Absolute Long	20(5/0)	24(6/0)	32(8/0)
d(PC)	Program Counter with Displacement	12(3/0)	16(4/0)	24(6/0)
d(PC, ix)	Program Counter with Index	14(3/0)	18(4/0)	26(6/0)
#xxx	Immediate	8(2/0)	8(2/0)	16(4/0)

*The size of the index register (ix) does not affect execution time.

E.3 MOVE INSTRUCTION EXECUTION TIMES

Tables E-2, E-3, and E-4 indicate the number of clock periods for the move instruction. This data includes instruction fetch, operand reads, and operand writes. The number of bus read and write cycles is shown in parenthesis as: (r/w).

Table E-2. Move Byte Instruction Execution Times

Source	Destination								
	Dn	An	(An)	(An) +	– (An)	d(An)	d(An, x)*	xxx.W	xxx.L
Dn	8(2/0)	8(2/0)	12(2/1)	12(2/1)	12(2/1)	20(4/1)	22(4/1)	20(4/1)	28(6/1)
An	8(2/0)	8(2/0)	12(2/1)	12(2/1)	12(2/1)	20(4/1)	22(4/1)	20(4/1)	28(6/1)
(An)	12(3/0)	12(3/0)	16(3/1)	16(3/1)	16(3/1)	24(5/1)	26(5/1)	24(5/1)	32(7/1)
(An) +	12(3/0)	12(3/0)	16(3/1)	16(3/1)	16(3/1)	24(5/1)	26(5/1)	24(5/1)	32(7/1)
– (An)	14(3/0)	14(3/0)	18(3/1)	18(3/1)	18(3/1)	26(5/1)	28(5/1)	26(5/1)	34(7/1)
d(An)	20(5/0)	20(5/0)	24(5/1)	24(5/1)	24(5/1)	32(7/1)	34(7/1)	32(7/1)	40(9/1)
d(An, ix)*	22(5/0)	22(5/0)	26(5/1)	26(5/1)	26(5/1)	34(7/1)	36(7/1)	34(7/1)	42(9/1)
xxx.W	20(5/0)	20(5/0)	24(5/1)	24(5/1)	24(5/1)	32(7/1)	34(7/1)	32(7/1)	40(9/1)
xxx.L	28(7/0)	28(7/0)	32(7/1)	32(7/1)	32(7/1)	40(9/1)	42(9/1)	40(9/1)	48(11/1)
d(PC)	20(5/0)	20(5/0)	24(5/1)	24(5/1)	24(5/1)	32(7/1)	34(7/1)	32(7/1)	40(9/1)
d(PC, ix)*	22(5/0)	22(5/0)	26(5/1)	26(5/1)	26(5/1)	34(7/1)	36(7/1)	34(7/1)	42(9/1)
#xxx	16(4/0)	16(4/0)	20(4/1)	20(4/1)	20(4/1)	28(6/1)	30(6/1)	28(6/1)	36(8/1)

*The size of the index register (ix) does not affect execution time.

Table E-3. Move Word Instruction Execution Times

Source	Destination								
	Dn	An	(An)	(An) +	– (An)	d(An)	d(An, ix)*	xxx.W	xxx.L
Dn	8(2/0)	8(2/0)	16(2/2)	16(2/2)	16(2/2)	24(4/2)	26(4/2)	20(4/2)	32(6/2)
An	8(2/0)	8(2/0)	16(2/2)	16(2/2)	16(2/2)	24(4/2)	26(4/2)	20(4/2)	32(6/2)
(An)	16(4/0)	16(4/0)	24(4/2)	24(4/2)	24(4/2)	32(6/2)	34(6/2)	32(6/2)	40(8/2)
(An) +	16(4/0)	16(4/0)	24(4/2)	24(4/2)	24(4/2)	32(6/2)	34(6/2)	32(6/2)	40(8/2)
– (An)	18(4/0)	18(4/0)	26(4/2)	26(4/2)	26(4/2)	34(6/2)	32(6/2)	34(6/2)	42(8/2)
d(An)	24(6/0)	24(6/0)	32(6/2)	32(6/2)	32(6/2)	40(8/2)	42(8/2)	40(8/2)	48(10/2)
d(An, ix)*	26(6/0)	26(6/0)	34(6/2)	34(6/2)	34(6/2)	42(8/2)	44(8/2)	42(8/2)	50(10/2)
xxx.W	24(6/0)	24(6/0)	32(6/2)	32(6/2)	32(6/2)	40(8/2)	42(8/2)	40(8/2)	48(10/2)
xxx.L	32(8/0)	32(8/0)	40(8/2)	40(8/2)	40(8/2)	48(10/2)	50(10/2)	48(10/2)	56(12/2)
d(PC)	24(6/0)	24(6/0)	32(6/2)	32(6/2)	32(6/2)	40(8/2)	42(8/2)	40(8/2)	48(10/2)
d(PC, ix)*	26(6/0)	26(6/0)	34(6/2)	34(6/2)	34(6/2)	42(8/2)	44(8/2)	42(8/2)	50(10/2)
#xxx	16(4/0)	16(4/0)	24(4/2)	24(4/2)	24(4/2)	32(6/2)	34(6/2)	32(6/2)	40(8/2)

*The size of the index register (ix) does not affect execution time.

Table E-4. Move Long Instruction Execution Times

Source	Destination Dn	An	(An)	(An) +	− (An)	d(An)	d(An, ix)*	xxx.W	xxx.L
Dn	8(2/0)	8(2/0)	24(2/4)	24(2/4)	24(2/4)	32(4/4)	34(4/4)	32(4/4)	40(6/4)
An	8(2/0)	8(2/0)	24(2/4)	24(2/4)	24(2/4)	32(4/4)	34(4/4)	32(4/4)	40(6/4)
(An)	24(6/0)	24(6/0)	40(6/4)	40(6/4)	40(6/4)	48(8/4)	50(8/4)	48(8/4)	56(10/4)
(An) +	24(6/0)	24(6/0)	40(6/4)	40(6/4)	40(6/4)	48(8/4)	50(8/4)	48(8/4)	56(10/4)
− (An)	26(6/0)	26(6/0)	42(6/4)	42(6/4)	42(6/4)	50(8/4)	52(8/4)	50(8/4)	58(10/4)
d(An)	32(8/0)	32(8/0)	48(8/4)	48(8/4)	48(8/4)	56(10/4)	58(10/4)	56(10/4)	64(12/4)
d(An, ix)*	34(8/0)	34(8/0)	50(8/4)	50(8/4)	50(8/4)	58(10/4)	60(10/4)	58(10/4)	66(12/4)
xxx.W	32(8/0)	32(8/0)	48(8/4)	48(8/4)	48(8/4)	56(10/4)	58(10/4)	56(10/4)	64(12/4)
xxx.L	40(10/0)	40(10/0)	56(10/4)	56(10/4)	56(10/4)	64(12/4)	66(12/4)	64(12/4)	72(14/4)
d(PC)	32(8/0)	32(8/0)	48(8/4)	48(8/4)	48(8/4)	56(10/4)	58(10/4)	56(10/4)	64(12/4)
d(PC, ix)*	34(8/0)	34(8/0)	50(8/4)	50(8/4)	50(8/4)	58(10/4)	60(10/4)	58(10/4)	66(12/4)
#xxx	24(6/0)	24(6/0)	40(6/4)	40(6/4)	40(6/4)	48(8/4)	50(8/4)	48(8/4)	56(10/4)

*The size of the index register (ix) does not affect execution time.

E.4 STANDARD INSTRUCTION EXECUTION TIMES

The number of clock periods shown in Table E-5 indicates the time required to perform the operations, store the results, and read the next instruction. The number of bus read and write cycles is shown in parenthesis as: (r/w). The number of clock periods and the number of read and write cycles must be added respectively to those of the effective address calculation where indicated. In Table E-5 the headings have the following meanings: An = address register operand, Dn = data register operand, ea = an operand specified by an effective address, and M = memory effective address operand.

Table E-5. Standard Instruction Execution Times

Instruction	Size	op <ea>, An	op <ea>, Dn	op Dn, <M>
ADD	Byte	—	8(2/0) +	12(2/1) +
	Word	12(2/0) +	8(2/0) +	16(2/2) +
	Long	10(2/0) + **	10(2/0) + **	24(2/4) +
AND	Byte	—	8(2/0) +	12(2/1) +
	Word	—	8(2/0) +	16(2/2) +
	Long	—	10(2/0) + **	24(2/4) +
CMP	Byte	—	8(2/0) +	—
	Word	10(2/0) +	8(2/0) +	—
	Long	10(2/0) +	10(2/0) +	—
DIVS		—	162(2/0) + *	—
DIVU		—	144(2/0) + *	—
EOR	Byte	—	8(2/0) + ***	12(2/1) +
	Word	—	8(2/0) + ***	16(2/2) +
	Long	—	12(2/0) + ***	24(2/4) +
MULS		—	74(2/0) + *	—
MULU		—	74(2/0) + *	—
OR	Byte	—	8(2/0) +	12(2/1) +
	Word	—	8(2/0) +	16(2/2) +
	Long	—	10(2/0) + **	24(2/4) +
SUB	Byte	—	8(2/0) +	12(2/1) +
	Word	12(2/0) +	8(2/0) +	16(2/2) +
	Long	10(2/0) + **	10(2/0) + **	24(2/4) +

NOTES:
- **+**   Add effective address calculation time
- *****   Indicates maximum value
- ******   The base time of 10 clock periods is increased to 12 if the effective address mode is register direct or immediate (effective address time should also be added).
- *******   Only available effective address mode is data register direct

DIVS, DIVU — The divide algorithm used by the MC68008 provides less than 10% difference between the best and worst case timings.

MULS, MULU — The multiply algorithm requires 42 + 2n clocks where n is defined as:
MULS: n = tag the <ea> with a zero as the MSB; n is the resultant number of 10 or 01 patterns in the 17-bit source, i.e., worst case happens when the source is $5555.
MULU: n = the number of ones in the <ea>

E.5 IMMEDIATE INSTRUCTION EXECUTION TIMES

The number of clock periods shown in Table E-6 includes the time to fetch immediate operands, perform the operations, store the results, and read the next operation. The number of bus read and write cycles is shown in parenthesis as: (r/w). The number of clock periods and the number of read and write cycles must be added respectively to those of the effective address calculation where indicated. In Table E-6, the headings have the following meanings: # = immediate operand, Dn = data register operand, An = address register operand, and M = memory operand.

Table E-6. Immediate Instruction Clock Periods

Instruction	Size	op#, Dn	op#, An	op#, M
ADDI	Byte	16(4/0)	—	20(4/1) +
	Word	16(4/0)	—	24(4/2) +
	Long	28(6/0)	—	40(6/4) +
ADDQ	Byte	8(2/0)	—	12(2/1) +
	Word	8(2/0)	12(2/0)	16(2/2) +
	Long	12(2/0)	12(2/0)	24(2/4) +
ANDI	Byte	16(4/0)	—	20(4/1) +
	Word	16(4/0)	—	24(4/2) +
	Long	28(6/0)	—	40(6/4) +
CMPI	Byte	16(4/0)	—	16(4/0) +
	Word	16(4/0)	—	16(4/0) +
	Long	26(6/0)	—	24(6/0) +
EORI	Byte	16(4/0)	—	20(4/1) +
	Word	16(4/0)	—	24(4/2) +
	Long	28(6/0)	—	40(6/4) +
MOVEQ	Long	8(2/0)	—	—
ORI	Byte	16(4/0)	—	20(4/1) +
	Word	16(4/0)	—	24(4/2) +
	Long	28(6/0)	—	40(6/4) +
SUBI	Byte	16(4/0)	—	12(2/1) +
	Word	16(4/0)	—	16(2/2) +
	Long	28(6/0)	—	24(2/4) +
SUBQ	Byte	8(2/0)	—	20(4/1) +
	Word	8(2/0)	12(2/0)	24(4/2) +
	Long	12(2/0)	12(2/0)	40(6/4) +

+ add effective address calculation time

E.6 SINGLE OPERAND INSTRUCTION EXECUTION TIMES

Table E-7 indicates the number of clock periods for the single operand instructions. The number of bus read and write cycles is shown in parenthesis as (r/w). The number of clock periods and the number of read and write cycles must be added respectively to those of the effective address calculation where indicated.

Table E-7. Single Operand Instruction Execution Times

Instruction	Size	Register	Memory
CLR	Byte	8(2/0)	12(2/1) +
	Word	8(2/0)	16(2/2) +
	Long	10(2/0)	24(2/4) +
NBCD	Byte	10(2/0)	12(2/1) +
NEG	Byte	8(2/0)	12(2/1) +
	Word	8(2/0)	16(2/2) +
	Long	10(2/0)	24(2/4) +
NEGX	Byte	8(2/0)	12(2/1) +
	Word	8(2/0)	16(2/2) +
	Long	10(2/0)	24(2/4) +
NOT	Byte	8(2/0)	12(2/1) +
	Word	8(2/0)	16(2/2) +
	Long	10(2/0)	24(2/4) +
S_{CC}	Byte, False	8(2/0)	12(2/1) +
	Byte, True	10(2/0)	12(2/1) +
TAS	Byte	8(2/0)	14(2/1) +
TST	Byte	8(2/0)	8(2/0) +
	Word	8(2/0)	8(2/0) +
	Long	8(2/0)	8(2/0) +

+ add effective address calculation time.

E.7 SHIFT/ROTATE INSTRUCTION EXECUTION TIMES

Table E-8 indicates the number of clock periods for the shift and rotate instructions. The number of bus read and write cycles is shown in parenthesis as: (r/w). The number of clock periods and the number of read and write cycles must be added respectively to those of the effective address calculation where indicated.

Table E-8. Shift/Rotate Instruction Clock Periods

Instruction	Size	Register	Memory
ASR, ASL	Byte	10 + 2n(2/0)	—
	Word	10 + 2n(2/0)	16(2/2) +
	Long	12 + 2n(2/0)	—
LSR, LSL	Byte	10 + 2n(2/0)	—
	Word	10 + 2n(2/0)	16(2/2) +
	Long	12 + 2n(2/0)	—
ROR, ROL	Byte	10 + 2n(2/0)	—
	Word	10 + 2n(2/0)	16(2/2) +
	Long	12 + 2n(2/0)	—
ROXR, ROXL	Byte	10 + 2n(2/0)	—
	Word	10 + 2n(2/0)	16(2/2) +
	Long	12 + 2n(2/0)	—

+ add effective address calculation time
n is the shift count

E.8 BIT MANIPULATION INSTRUCTION EXECUTION TIMES

Table E-9 indicates the number of clock periods required for the bit manipulation instructions. The number of bus read and write cycles is shown in parenthesis as: (r/w). The number of clock periods and the number of read and write cycles must be added respectively to those of the effective address calculation where indicated.

Table E-9. Bit Manipulation Instruction Execution Times

Instruction	Size	Dynamic		Static	
		Register	Memory	Register	Memory
BCHG	Byte	—	12(2/1) +	—	20(4/1) +
	Long	12(2/0)*	—	20(4/0)*	—
BCLR	Byte	—	12(2/1) +	—	20(4/1) +
	Long	14(2/0)*	—	22(4/0)*	—
BSET	Byte	—	12(2/1) +	—	20(4/1) +
	Long	12(2/0)*	—	20(4/0)*	—
BTST	Byte	—	8(2/0) +	—	16(4/0) +
	Long	10(2/0)	—	18(4/0)	—

+ add effective address calculation time
* indicates maximum value

E.9 CONDITIONAL INSTRUCTION EXECUTION TIMES

Table E-10 indicates the number of clock periods required for the conditional instructions. The number of bus read and write cycles is indicated in parenthesis as: (r/w). The number of clock periods and the number of read and write cycles must be added respectively to those of the effective address calculation where indicated.

Table E-10. Conditional Instruction Execution Times

Instruction	Displacement	Trap or Branch Taken	Trap or Branch Not Taken
B$_{CC}$	Byte	18(4/0)	12(2/0)
	Word	18(4/0)	20(4/0)
BRA	Byte	18(4/0)	—
	Word	18(4/0)	—
BSR	Byte	34(4/4)	—
	Word	34(4/4)	—
DBCC	CC True	—	20(4/0)
	CC False	18(4/0)	26(6/0)
CHK	—	68(8/6) + *	14(2/0) +
TRAP	—	62(8/6)	—
TRAPV	—	66(10/6)	8(2/0)

+ add effective address calculation time
* indicates maximum value

E.10 JMP, JSR, LEA, PEA, AND MOVEM INSTRUCTION EXECUTION TIMES

Table E-11 indicates the number of clock periods required for the jump, jump-to-subroutine, load effective address, push effective address, and move multiple registers instructions. The number of bus read and write cycles is shown in parenthesis as: (r/w).

Table E-11. JMP, JSR, LEA, PEA, and MOVEM Instruction Execution Times

Instruction	Size	(An)	(An) +	– (An)	d(An)	d(An, ix) *	xxx.W	xxx.L
JMP	–	16(4/0)	–	–	18(4/0)	22(4/0)	18(4/0)	24(6/0)
JSR	–	32(4/4)	–	–	34(4/4)	38(4/4)	34(4/4)	40(6/4)
LEA	–	8(2/0)	–	–	16(4/0)	20(4/0)	16(4/0)	24(6/0)
PEA	–	24(2/4)	–	–	32(4/4)	36(4/4)	32(4/4)	40(6/4)
MOVEM M → R	Word	24 + 8n (6 + 2n/0)	24 + 8n (6 + 2n/0)	–	32 + 8n (8 + 2n/0)	34 + 8n (8 + 2n/0)	32 + 8n (10 + n/0)	40 + 8n (10 + 2n/0)
	Long	24 + 16n (6 + 4n/0)	24 + 16n (6 + 4n/0)	–	32 + 16n (8 + 4n/0)	32 + 16n (8 + 4n/0)	32 + 16n (8 + 4n/0)	40 + 16n (8 + 4n/0)
MOVEM R → M	Word	16 + 8n (4/2n)	–	16 + 8n (4/2n)	24 + 8n (6/2n)	26 + 8n (6/2n)	24 + 8n (6/2n)	32 + 8n (8/2n)
	Long	16 + 16n (4/4n)	–	16 + 16n (4/4n)	24 + 16n (6/4n)	26 + 16n	24 + 16n (8/4n)	32 + 16n (6/4n)

n is the number of registers to move
* is the size of the index register (ix) does not affect the instruction's execution time

E.11 MULTI-PRECISION INSTRUCTION EXECUTION TIMES

Table E-12 indicates the number of clock periods for the multi-precision instructions. The number of clock periods includes the time to fetch both operands, perform the operations, store the results, and read the next instructions. The number of read and write cycles is shown in parenthesis as: (r/w).

In Table E-12, the headings have the following meanings: Dn = data register operand and M = memory operand.

Table E-12. Multi-Precision Instruction Execution Times

Instruction	Size	op Dn, Dn	op M, M
ADDX	Byte	8(2/0)	22(4/1)
	Word	8(2/0)	50(6/2)
	Long	12(2/0)	58(10/4)
CMPM	Byte	–	16(4/0)
	Word	–	24(6/0)
	Long	–	40(10/0)
SUBX	Byte	8(2/0)	22(4/1)
	Word	8(2/0)	50(6/2)
	Long	12(2/0)	58(10/4)
ABCD	Byte	10(2/0)	20(4/1)
SBCD	Byte	10(2/0)	20(4/1)

MC68008

E.12 MISCELLANEOUS INSTRUCTION EXECUTION TIMES

Tables E-13 and E-14 indicate the number of clock periods for the following miscellaneous instructions. The number of bus read and write cycles is shown in parenthesis as: (r/w). The number of clock periods plus the number of read and write cycles must be added to those of the effective address calculation where indicated.

Table E-13. Miscellaneous Instruction Execution Times

Instruction	Register	Memory
ANDI to CCR	32(6/0)	—
ANDI to SR	32(6/0)	—
EORI to CCR	32(6/0)	—
EORI to SR	32(6/0)	—
EXG	10(2/0)	—
EXT	8(2/0)	—
LINK	32(4/4)	—
MOVE to CCR	18(4/0)	18(4/0) +
MOVE to SR	18(4/0)	18(4/0) +
MOVE from SR	10(2/0)	16(2/2) +
MOVE to USP	8(2/0)	—
MOVE from USP	8(2/0)	—
NOP	8(2/0)	—
ORI to CCR	32(6/0)	—
ORI to SR	32(6/0)	—
RESET	136(2/0)	—
RTE	40(10/0)	—
RTR	40(10/0)	—
RTS	32(8/0)	—
STOP	4(0/0)	—
SWAP	8(2/0)	—
UNLK	24(6/0)	—

+ add effective address calculation time

Table E-14. Move Peripheral Instruction Execution Times

Instruction	Size	Register → Memory	Memory → Register
MOVEP	Word	24(4/2)	24(6/0)
	Long	32(4/4)	32(8/0)

+ add effective address calculation time

E.13 EXCEPTION PROCESSING EXECUTION TIMES

Table E-15 indicates the number of clock periods for exception processing. The number of clock periods includes the time for all stacking, the vector fetch, and the fetch of the first instruction of the handler routine. The number of bus read and write cycles is shown in parenthesis as: (r/w).

Table E-15. Exception Processing Execution Times

Exception	Periods
Address Error	**94**(8/14)
Bus Error	**94**(8/14)
Interrupt	**72**(9/6)*
Illegal Instruction	**62**(8/6)
Privileged Instruction	**62**(8/6)
Trace	**62**(8/6)

*The interrupt acknowledge bus cycle is assumed to take four external clock periods.

MC68008

APPENDIX F
MC68010 INSTRUCTION EXECUTION TIMES

F.1 INTRODUCTION

This Appendix contains listings of the instruction execution times in terms of external clock (CLK) periods. In this data, it is assumed that both memory read and write cycle times are four clock periods. A longer memory cycle will cause the generation of wait states which must be added to the total instruction time.

The number of bus read and write cycles for each instruction is also included with the timing data. This data is enclosed in parenthesis following the number of clock periods and is shown as: (r/w) where r is the number of read cycles and w is the number of write cycles included in the clock period number. Recalling that either a read or write cycle requires four clock periods, a timing number given as 18(3/1) relates to 12 clock periods for the three read cycles, plus 4 clock periods for the one write cycle, plus 2 cycles required for some internal function of the processor.

NOTE
The number of periods includes instruction fetch and all applicable operand fetches and stores.

F.2 OPERAND EFFECTIVE ADDRESS CALCULATION TIMES

Table F-1 lists the number of clock periods required to compute an instruction's effective address. It includes fetching of any extension words, the address computation, and fetching of the memory operand if necessary. Several instructions do not need the operand at an effective address to be fetched and thus require fewer clock periods to calculate a given effective address than the instructions that do fetch the effective address operand. The number of bus read and write cycles is shown in parenthesis as (r/w). Note there are no write cycles involved in processing the effective address.

Table F-1. Effective Address Calculation Times

Addressing Mode		Byte, Word		Long	
		Fetch	No Fetch	Fetch	No Fetch
	Register				
Dn	Data Register Direct	0(0/0)	—	0(0/0)	—
An	Address Register Direct	0(0/0)	—	0(0/0)	—
	Memory				
(An)	Address Register Indirect	4(1/0)	2(0/0)	8(2/0)	2(0/0)
(An)+	Address Register Indirect with Postincrement	4(1/0)	4(0/0)	8(2/0)	4(0/0)
−(An)	Address Register Indirect with Predecrement	6(1/0)	4(0/0)	10(2/0)	4(0/0)
d(An)	Address Register Indirect with Displacement	8(2/0)	4(0/0)	12(3/0)	4(1/0)
d(An, ix)*	Address Register Indirect with Index	10(2/0)	8(1/0)	14(3/0)	8(1/0)
xxx.W	Absolute Short	8(2/0)	4(1/0)	12(3/0)	4(1/0)
xxx.L	Absolute Long	12(3/0)	8(2/0)	16(4/0)	8(2/0)
d(PC)	Program Counter with Displacement	8(2/0)	—	12(3/0)	—
d(PC, ix)	Program Counter with Index	10(2/0)	—	14(3/0)	—
#xxx	Immediate	4(1/0)	—	8(2/0)	—

*The size of the index register (ix) does not affect execution time.

F.3 MOVE INSTRUCTION EXECUTION TIMES

Tables F-2, F-3, F-4, and F-5 indicate the number of clock periods for the move instruction. This data includes instruction fetch, operand reads, and operand writes. The number of bus read and write cycles is shown in parenthesis as (r/w).

Table F-2. Move Byte and Word Instruction Execution Times

Source	Destination								
	Dn	An	(An)	(An)+	−(An)	d(An)	d(An, ix)*	xxx.W	xxx.L
Dn	4(1/0)	4(1/0)	8(1/1)	8(1/1)	8(1/1)	12(2/1)	14(2/1)	12(2/1)	16(3/1)
An	4(1/0)	4(1/0)	8(1/1)	8(1/1)	8(1/1)	12(2/1)	14(2/1)	12(2/1)	16(3/1)
(An)	8(2/0)	8(2/0)	12(2/1)	12(2/1)	12(2/1)	16(3/1)	18(3/1)	16(3/1)	20(4/1)
(An)+	8(2/0)	8(2/0)	12(2/1)	12(2/1)	12(2/1)	16(3/1)	18(3/1)	16(3/1)	20(4/1)
−(An)	10(2/0)	10(2/0)	14(2/1)	14(2/1)	14(2/1)	18(3/1)	20(3/1)	18(3/1)	22(4/1)
d(An)	12(3/0)	12(3/0)	16(3/1)	16(3/1)	16(3/1)	20(4/1)	22(4/1)	20(4/1)	24(5/1)
d(An, ix)*	14(3/0)	14(3/0)	18(3/1)	18(3/1)	18(3/1)	22(4/1)	24(4/1)	22(4/1)	26(5/1)
xxx.W	12(3/0)	12(3/0)	16(3/1)	16(3/1)	16(3/1)	20(4/1)	22(4/1)	20(4/1)	24(5/1)
xxx.L	16(4/0)	16(4/0)	20(4/1)	20(4/1)	20(4/1)	24(5/1)	26(5/1)	24(5/1)	28(6/1)
d(PC)	12(3/0)	12(3/0)	16(3/1)	16(3/1)	16(3/1)	20(4/1)	22(4/1)	20(4/1)	24(5/1)
d(PC, ix)*	14(3/0)	14(3/0)	18(3/1)	18(3/1)	18(3/1)	22(4/1)	24(4/1)	22(4/1)	26(5/1)
#xxx	8(2/0)	8(2/0)	12(2/1)	12(2/1)	12(2/1)	16(3/1)	18(3/1)	16(3/1)	20(4/1)

*The size of the index register (ix) does not affect execution time.

Table F-3. Move Byte and Word Instruction Loop Mode Execution Times

	Loop Continued			Loop Terminated					
	Valid Count, cc False			Valid Count, cc True			Expired Count		
Source	Destination								
	(An)	(An)+	−(An)	(An)	(An)+	−(An)	(An)	(An)+	−(An)
Dn	10(0/1)	10(0/1)	—	18(2/1)	18(2/1)	—	16(2/1)	16(2/1)	—
An*	10(0/1)	10(0/1)	—	18(2/1)	18(2/1)	—	16(2/1)	16(2/1)	—
(An)	14(1/1)	14(1/1)	16(1/1)	20(3/1)	20(3/1)	22(3/1)	18(3/1)	18(3/1)	20(3/1)
(An)+	14(1/1)	14(1/1)	16(1/1)	20(3/1)	20(3/1)	22(3/1)	18(3/1)	18(3/1)	20(3/1)
−(An)	16(1/1)	16(1/1)	18(1/1)	22(3/1)	22(3/1)	24(3/1)	20(3/1)	20(3/1)	22(3/1)

*Word only.

Table F-4. Move Long Instruction Execution Times

Source	Destination								
	Dn	An	(An)	(An)+	−(An)	d(An)	d(An, ix)*	xxx.W	xxx.L
Dn	4(1/0)	4(1/0)	12(1/2)	12(1/2)	14(1/2)	16(2/2)	18(2/2)	16(2/2)	20(3/2)
An	4(1/0)	4(1/0)	12(1/2)	12(1/2)	14(1/2)	16(2/2)	18(2/2)	16(2/2)	20(3/2)
(An)	12(3/0)	12(3/0)	20(3/2)	20(3/2)	20(3/2)	24(4/2)	26(4/2)	24(4/2)	28(5/2)
(An)+	12(3/0)	12(3/0)	20(3/2)	20(3/2)	20(3/2)	24(4/2)	26(4/2)	24(4/2)	28(5/2)
−(An)	14(3/0)	14(3/0)	22(3/2)	22(3/2)	22(3/2)	26(4/2)	28(4/2)	26(4/2)	30(5/2)
d(An)	16(4/0)	16(4/0)	24(4/2)	24(4/2)	24(4/2)	28(5/2)	30(5/2)	28(5/2)	32(6/2)
d(An, ix)*	18(4/0)	18(4/0)	26(4/2)	26(4/2)	26(4/2)	30(5/2)	32(5/2)	30(5/2)	34(6/2)
xxx.W	16(4/0)	16(4/0)	24(4/2)	24(4/2)	24(4/2)	28(5/2)	30(5/2)	28(5/2)	32(6/2)
xxx.L	20(5/0)	20(5/0)	28(5/2)	28(5/2)	28(5/2)	32(6/2)	34(6/2)	32(6/2)	36(7/2)
d(PC)	16(4/0)	16(4/0)	24(4/2)	24(4/2)	24(4/2)	28(5/2)	30(5/2)	28(5/2)	32(5/2)
d(PC, ix)*	18(4/0)	18(4/0)	26(4/2)	26(4/2)	26(4/2)	30(5/2)	32(5/2)	30(5/2)	34(6/2)
#xxx	12(3/0)	12(3/0)	20(3/2)	20(3/2)	20(3/2)	24(4/2)	26(4/2)	24(4/2)	28(5/2)

*The size of the index register (ix) does not affect execution time.

MC68010

	Loop Continued			Loop Terminated					
	Valid Count, cc False			Valid Count, cc True			Expired Count		
				Destination					
Source	(An)	(An)+	−(An)	(An)	(An)+	−(An)	(An)	(An)+	−(An)
Dn	14(0/2)	14(0/2)	−	20(2/2)	20(2/2)	−	18(2/2)	18(2/2)	−
An	14(0/2)	14(0/2)	−	20(2/2)	20(2/2)	−	18(2/2)	18(2/2)	−
(An)	22(2/2)	22(2/2)	24(2/2)	28(4/2)	28(4/2)	30(4/2)	24(4/2)	24(4/2)	26(4/2)
(An)+	22(2/2)	22(2/2)	24(2/2)	28(4/2)	28(4/2)	30(4/2)	24(4/2)	24(4/2)	26(4/2)
−(An)	24(2/2)	24(2/2)	26(2/2)	30(4/2)	30(4/2)	32(4/2)	26(4/2)	26(4/2)	28(4/2)

F.4 STANDARD INSTRUCTION EXECUTION TIMES

The number of clock periods shown in Tables F-6 and F-7 indicate the time required to perform the operations, store the results, and read the next instruction. The number of bus read and write cycles is shown in parenthesis as (r/w). The number of clock periods and the number of read and write cycles must be added respectively to those of the effective address calculation where indicated.

In Tables F-6 and F-7 the headings have the following meanings: An = address register operand, Dn = data register operand, ea = an operand specified by an effective address, and M = memory effective address operand.

Table F-6. Standard Instruction Execution Times

Instruction	Size	op<ea>, An***	op<ea>, Dn	op Dn, <M>
ADD	Byte, Word	8(1/0)+	4(1/0)+	8(1/1)+
	Long	6(1/0)+	6(1/0)+	12(1/2)+
AND	Byte, Word	−	4(1/0)+	8(1/1)+
	Long	−	6(1/0)+	12(1/2)+
CMP	Byte, Word	6(1/0)+	4(1/0)+	−
	Long	6(1/0)+	6(1/0)+	−
DIVS	−	−	122(1/0)+	−
DIVU	−	−	108(1/0)+	−
EOR	Byte, Word	−	4(1/0)**	8(1/1)+
	Long	−	6(1/0)**	12(1/2)+
MULS	−	−	42(1/0)+*	−
MULU	−	−	40(1/0)+	−
OR	Byte, Word	−	4(1/0)+	8(1/1)+
	Long	−	6(1/0)+	12(1/2)+
SUB	Byte, Word	8(1/0)+	4(1/0)+	8(1/1)+
	Long	6(1/0)+	6(1/0)+	12(1/2)+

NOTES:
+   add effective address calculation time
*   indicates maximum value
**   only available addressing mode is data register direct
***   word or long only

MC68010

Table F-7. Standard Instruction Loop Mode Execution Times

Instruction	Size	Loop Continued			Loop Terminated					
		Valid Count cc False			Valid Count cc True			Expired Count		
		op <ea>, An*	op <ea>, Dn	op Dn, <ea>	op <ea>, An*	op <ea>, Dn	op Dn, <ea>	op <ea>, An*	op <ea>, Dn	op Dn, <ea>
ADD	Byte, Word	18(1/0)	16(1/0)	16(1/1)	24(3/0)	22(3/0)	22(3/1)	22(3/0)	20(3/0)	20(3/1)
	Long	22(2/0)	22(2/0)	24(2/2)	28(4/0)	28(4/0)	30(4/2)	26(4/0)	26(4/0)	28(4/2)
AND	Byte, Word	—	16(1/0)	16(1/1)	—	22(3/0)	22(3/1)	—	20(3/0)	20(3/1)
	Long	—	22(2/0)	24(2/2)	—	28(4/0)	30(4/2)	—	26(4/0)	28(4/2)
CMP	Byte, Word	12(1/0)	12(1/0)	—	18(3/0)	18(3/0)	—	16(3/0)	16(4/0)	—
	Long	18(2/0)	18(2/0)	—	24(4/0)	24(4/0)	—	20(4/0)	20(4/0)	—
EOR	Byte, Word	—	—	16(1/0)	—	—	22(3/1)	—	—	20(3/1)
	Long	—	—	24(2/2)	—	—	30(4/2)	—	—	28(4/2)
OR	Byte, Word	—	16(1/0)	16(1/0)	—	22(3/0)	22(3/1)	—	20(3/0)	20(3/1)
	Long	—	22(2/0)	24(2/2)	—	28(4/0)	30(4/2)	—	26(4/0)	28(4/2)
SUB	Byte, Word	18(1/0)	16(1/0)	16(1/1)	24(3/0)	22(3/0)	22(3/1)	22(3/0)	20(3/0)	20(3/1)
	Long	22(2/0)	20(2/0)	24(2/2)	28(4/0)	26(4/0)	30(4/2)	26(4/0)	24(4/0)	28(4/2)

*Word or long only.
<ea> may be (An), +(An), or −(An) only. Add two clock periods to the table value if <ea> is −(An).

F.5 IMMEDIATE INSTRUCTION EXECUTION TIMES

The number of clock periods shown in Table F-8 includes the time to fetch immediate operands, perform the operations, store the results, and read the next operation. The number of bus read and write cycles is shown in parenthesis as (r/w). The number of clock periods and the number of read and write cycles must be added respectively to those of the effective address calculation where indicated.

In Table F-8, the headings have the following meanings: # = immediate operand, Dn = data register operand, An = address register operand, and M = memory operand.

Table F-8 Immediate Instruction Execution Times

Instruction	Size	op #, Dn	op #, An	op #, M
ADDI	Byte, Word	8(2/0)	—	12(2/1) +
	Long	14(3/0)	—	20(3/2) +
ADDQ	Byte, Word	4(1/0)	4(1/0) *	8(1/1) +
	Long	8(1/0)	8(1/0)	12(1/2) +
ANDI	Byte, Word	8(2/0)	—	12(2/1) +
	Long	14(3/0)	—	20(3/1) +
CMPI	Byte, Word	8(2/0)	—	8(2/0) +
	Long	12(3/0)	—	12(3/0) +
EORI	Byte, Word	8(2/0)	—	12(2/1) +
	Long	14(3/0)	—	20(3/2) +
MOVEQ	Long	4(1/0)	—	—
ORI	Byte, Word	8(2/0)	—	12(2/1) +
	Long	14(3/0)	—	20(3/2) +
SUBI	Byte, Word	8(2/0)	—	12(2/1) +
	Long	14(3/0)	—	20(3/2) +
SUBQ	Byte, Word	4(1/0)	4(1/0) *	8(1/1) +
	Long	8(1/0)	8(1/0)	12(1/2) +

+ add effective address calculation time.
* word only

F.6 SINGLE OPERAND INSTRUCTION EXECUTION TIMES

Tables F-9, F-10, and F-11 indicate the number of clock periods for the single operand instructions. The number of bus read and write cycles is shown in parenthesis as (r/w). The number of clock periods and the number of read and write cycles must be added respectively to those of the effective address calculation where indicated.

Table F-9. Single Operand Instruction Execution Times

Instruction	Size	Register	Memory
NBCD	Byte	6(1/0)	8(1/1) +
NEG	Byte, Word	4(1/0)	8(1/1) +
	Long	6(1/0)	12(1/2) +
NEGX	Byte, Word	4(1/0)	8(1/1) +
	Long	6(1/0)	12(1/2) +
NOT	Byte, Word	4(1/0)	8(1/1) +
	Long	6(1/0)	12(1/2) +
Scc	Byte, False	4(1/0)	8(1/1) + *
	Byte, True	4(1/0)	8(1/1) + *
TAS	Byte	4(1/0)	14(2/1) + *
TST	Byte, Word	4(1/0)	4(1/0)
	Long	4(1/0)	4(1/0) +

+ add effective address calculation time
* Use non-fetching effective address calculation time.

Table F-10. Clear Instruction Execution Times

	Size	Dn	An	(An)	(An) +	− (An)	d(An)	d(An, ix) *	xxx.W	xxx.L
CLR	Byte, Word	4(1/0)	—	8(1/1)	8(1/1)	10(1/1)	12(2/1)	16(2/1)	12(2/1)	16(3/1)
	Long	6(1/0)	—	12(1/2)	12(1/2)	14(1/2)	16(2/2)	20(2/2)	16(2/2)	20(3/2)

* The size of the index register (ix) does not affect execution time.

Table F-11. Single Operand Instruction Loop Mode Execution Times

		Loop Continued			Loop Terminated					
		Valid Count, cc False			Valid Count, cc True			Expired Count		
Instruction	Size	(An)	(An) +	− (An)	(An)	(An) +	− (An)	(An)	(An) +	− (An)
CLR	Byte, Word	10(0/1)	10(0/1)	12(0/1)	18(2/1)	18(2/1)	20(2/0)	16(2/1)	16(2/1)	18(2/1)
	Long	14(0/2)	14(0/2)	16(0/2)	22(2/2)	22(2/2)	24(2/2)	20(2/2)	20(2/2)	22(2/2)
NBCD	Byte	18(1/1)	18(1/1)	20(1/1)	24(3/1)	24(3/1)	26(3/1)	22(3/1)	22(3/1)	24(3/1)
NEG	Byte, Word	16(1/1)	16(1/1)	18(2/2)	22(3/1)	22(3/1)	24(3/1)	20(3/1)	20(3/1)	22(3/1)
	Long	24(2/2)	24(2/2)	26(2/2)	30(4/2)	30(4/2)	32(4/2)	28(4/2)	28(4/2)	30(4/2)
NEGX	Byte, Word	16(1/1)	16(1/1)	18(2/2)	22(3/1)	22(3/1)	24(3/1)	20(3/1)	20(3/1)	22(3/1)
	Long	24(2/2)	24(2/2)	26(2/2)	30(4/2)	30(4/2)	32(4/2)	28(4/2)	28(4/2)	30(4/2)
NOT	Byte, Word	16(1/1)	16(1/1)	18(2/2)	22(3/1)	22(3/1)	24(3/1)	20(3/1)	20(3/1)	22(3/1)
	Long	24(2/2)	24(2/2)	26(2/2)	30(4/2)	30(4/2)	32(4/2)	28(4/2)	28(4/2)	30(4/2)
TST	Byte, Word	12(1/0)	12(1/0)	14(1/0)	18(3/0)	18(3/0)	20(3/0)	16(3/0)	16(3/0)	18(3/0)
	Long	18(2/0)	18(2/0)	20(2/0)	24(4/0)	24(4/0)	26(4/0)	20(4/0)	20(4/0)	22(4/0)

MC68010

211

F.7 SHIFT/ROTATE INSTRUCTION EXECUTION TIMES

Tables F-12 and F-13 indicate the number of clock periods for the shift and rotate instructions. The number of bus read and write cycles is shown in parenthesis as (r/w). The number of clock periods and the number of read and write cycles must be added respectively to those of the effective address calculation where indicated.

Table F-12. Shift/Rotate Instruction Execution Times

Instruction	Size	Register	Memory*
ASR, ASL	Byte, Word	6 + 2n(1/0)	8(1/1) +
	Long	8 + 2n(1/0)	—
LSR, LSL	Byte, Word	6 + 2n(1/0)	8(1/1) +
	Long	8 + 2n(1/0)	—
ROR, ROL	Byte, Word	6 + 2n(1/0)	8(1/1) +
	Long	8 + 2n(1/0)	—
ROXR, ROXL	Byte, Word	6 + 2n(1/0)	8(1/1) +
	Long	8 + 2n(1/0)	—

+ add effective address calculation time
n is the shift or rotate count
* word only

Table F-13. Shift/Rotate Instruction Loop Mode Execution Times

Instruction	Size	Loop Continued			Loop Terminated					
		Valid Count, cc False			Valid Count, cc True			Expired Count		
		(An)	(An) +	− (An)	(An)	(An) +	− (An)	(An)	(An) +	− (An)
ASR, ASL	Word	18(1/1)	18(1/1)	20(1/1)	24(3/1)	24(3/1)	26(3/1)	22(3/1)	22(3/1)	24(3/1)
LSR, LSL	Word	18(1/1)	18(1/1)	20(1/1)	24(3/1)	24(3/1)	26(3/1)	22(3/1)	22(3/1)	24(3/1)
ROR, ROL	Word	18(1/1)	18(1/1)	20(1/1)	24(3/1)	24(3/1)	26(3/1)	22(3/1)	22(3/1)	24(3/1)
ROXR, ROXL	Word	18(1/1)	18(1/1)	20(1/1)	24(3/1)	24(3/1)	26(3/1)	22(3/1)	22(3/1)	24(3/1)

MC68010

F.8 BIT MANIPULATION INSTRUCTION EXECUTION TIMES

Table F-14 indicates the number of clock periods required for the bit manipulation instructions. The number of bus read and write cycles is shown in parenthesis as (r/w). The number of clock periods and the number of read and write cycles must be added respectively to those of the effective address calculation where indicated.

Table F-14. Bit Manipulation Instruction Execution Times

Instruction	Size	Dynamic		Static	
		Register	Memory	Register	Memory
BCHG	Byte	—	8(1/1) +	—	12(2/1) +
	Long	8(1/0) *	—	12(2/0) *	—
BCLR	Byte	—	10(1/1) +	—	14(2/1) +
	Long	10(1/0) *	—	14(2/0) *	—
BSET	Byte	—	8(1/1) +	—	12(2/1) +
	Long	8(1/0) *	—	12(2/0) *	—
BTST	Byte	—	4(1/0) +	—	8(2/0) +
	Long	6(1/0) *	—	10(2/0)	—

+ add effective address calculation time
* indicates maximum value

F.9 CONDITIONAL INSTRUCTION EXECUTION TIMES

Table F-15 indicates the number of clock periods required for the conditional instructions. The number of bus read and write cycles is indicated in parenthesis as (r/w). The number of clock periods and the number of read and write cycles must be added respectively to those of the effective address calculation where indicated.

Table F-15. Conditional Instruction Execution Times

Instruction	Displacement	Branch Taken	Branch Not Taken
BCC	Byte	10(2/0)	6(1/0)
	Word	10(2/0)	10(2/0)
BRA	Byte	10(2/0)	—
	Word	10(2/0)	—
BSR	Byte	18(2/2)	—
	Word	18(2/2)	—
DBCC	CC true	—	10(2/0)
	CC false	10(2/0)	16(3/0)

+ add effective address calculation time
* indicates maximum value

F.10 JMP, JSR, LEA, PEA, AND MOVEM INSTRUCTION EXECUTION TIMES

Table F-16 indicates the number of clock periods required for the jump, jump-to-subroutine, load effective address, push effective address, and move multiple registers instructions. The number of bus read and write cycles is shown in parenthesis as (r/w).

Table F-16. JMP, JSR, LEA, PEA, and MOVEM Instruction Execution Times

Instr	Size	(An)	(An) +	− (An)	d(An)	d(An, ix) +	xxx.W	xxx.L	d(PC)	d(PC, ix) *
JMP	—	8(2/0)	—	—	10(2/0)	14(3/0)	10(2/0)	12(3/0)	10(2/0)	14(3/0)
JSR	—	16(2/2)	—	—	18(2/2)	22(2/2)	18(2/2)	20(3/2)	18(2/2)	22(2/2)
LEA	—	4(1/0)	—	—	8(2/0)	12(2/0)	8(2/0)	12(3/0)	8(2/0)	12(2/0)
PEA	—	12(1/2)	—	—	16(2/2)	20(2/2)	16(2/2)	20(3/2)	16(2/2)	20(2/2)
MOVEM M → R	Word	12 + 4n (3 + n/0)	12 + 4n (3 + n/0)	—	16 + 4n (4 + n/0)	18 + 4n (4 + n/0)	16 + 4n (4 + n/0)	20 + 4n (5 + n/0)	16 + 4n (4 + n/0)	18 + 4n (4 + n/0)
	Long	12 + 8n (3 + 2n/0)	12 + 8n (3 + 2n/0)	—	16 + 8n (4 + 2n/0)	18 + 8n (4 + 2n/0)	16 + 8n (4 + 2n/0)	20 + 8n (5 + 2n/0)	16 + 8n (4 + 2n/0)	18 + 8n (4 + 2n/0)
MOVEM R → M	Word	8 + 4n (2/n)	—	8 + 4n (2/n)	12 + 4n (3/n)	14 + 4n (3/n)	12 + 4n (3/n)	16 + 4n (4/n)	—	—
	Long	8 + 8n (2/2n)	—	8 + 8n (2/2n)	12 + 8n (3/2n)	14 + 8n (3/2n)	12 + 8n (3/2n)	16 + 8n (4/2n)	—	—

n is the number of registers to move
* is the size of the index register (ix) does not affect the instruction's execution time

F.11 MULTI-PRECISION INSTRUCTION EXECUTION TIMES

Table F-17 indicates the number of clock periods for the multi-precision instructions. The number of clock periods includes the time to fetch both operands, perform the operations, store the results, and read the next instructions. The number of read and write cycles is shown in parenthesis as (r/w).

In Table F-17, the headings have the following meanings: Dn = data register operand and M = memory operand.

Table F-17. Multi-Precision Instruction Execution Times

Instruction	Size	Non-Looped op Dn, Dn	Continued Valid Count, cc False	Terminated Valid Count, cc True	Terminated Expired Count
			op M, M*		
ADDX	Byte, Word	4(1/0)	18(3/10)	22(2/1)	28(4/1)	26(4/1)
	Long	6(1/0)	30(5/2)	32(4/2)	38(6/2)	36(6/2)
CMPM	Byte, Word	—	12(3/0)	14(2/0)	20(4/0)	18(4/0)
	Long	—	20(5/0)	24(4/0)	30(6/0)	26(6/0)
SUBX	Byte, Word	4(1/0)	18(3/1)	22(2/1)	28(4/1)	26(4/1)
	Long	6(1/0)	30(5/2)	32(4/2)	38(6/2)	36(6/2)
ABCD	Byte	6(1/0)	18(3/1)	24(2/1)	30(4/1)	28(4/1)
SBCD	Byte	6(1/0)	18(3/1)	24(2/1)	30(4/1)	28(4/1)

*Source and destination ea is (An)+ for CMPM and − (An) for all others.

MC68010

F.12 MISCELLANEOUS INSTRUCTION EXECUTION TIMES

Table F-18 indicates the number of clock periods for the following miscellaneous instructions. The number of bus read and write cycles is shown in parenthesis as (r/w). The number of clock periods plus the number of read and write cycles must be added to those of the effective address calculation where indicated.

Table F-18. Miscellaneous Instruction Execution Times

Instruction	Size	Register	Memory	Register → Destination**	Source** → Register
ANDI to CCR	—	16(2/0)	—	—	—
ANDI to SR	— '	16(2/0)	—	—	—
CHK	—	8(1/0) +	—	—	—
EORI to CCR	—	16(2/0)	—	—	—
EORI to SR	—	16(2/0)	—	—	—
EXG	—	6(1/0)	—	—	—
EXT	Word	4(1/0)	—	—	—
	Long	4(1/0)	—	—	—
LINK	—	16(2/2)	—	—	—
MOVE from CCR	—	4(1/0)	8(1/1) + *	—	—
MOVE to CCR	—	12(2/0)	12(2/0) +	—	—
MOVE from SR	—	4(1/0)	8(1/1) + *	—	—
MOVE to SR	—	12(2/0)	12(2/0) +	—	—
MOVE from USP	—	6(1/0)	—	—	—
MOVE to USP	—	6(1/0)	—	—	—
MOVEC	—	—	—	10(2/0)	12(2/0)
MOVEP	Word	—	—	16(2/2)	16(4/0)
	Long	—	—	24(2/4)	24(6/0)
NOP	—	4(1/0)	—	—	—
ORI to CCR	—	16(2/0)	—	—	—
ORI to SR	—	16(2/0)	—	—	—
RESET	—	130(1/0)	—	—	—
RTD	—	16(4/0)	—	—	—
RTE	Short	24(6/0)	—	—	—
	Long, Retry Read	112(27/10)	—	—	—
	Long, Retry Write	112(26/1)	—	—	—
	Long, No Retry	110(26/0)	—	—	—
RTR	—	20(5/0)	—	—	—
RTS	—	16(4/0)	—	—	—
STOP	—	4(0/0)	—	—	—
SWAP	—	4(1/0)	—	—	—
TRAPV	—	4(1/0)	—	—	—
UNLK	—	12(3/0)	—	—	—

\+ add effective address calculation time.
* use non-fetching effective address calculation time.
** Source or destination is a memory location for the MOVEP instruction and a control register for the MOVEC instruction.

MC68010

F.13 EXCEPTION PROCESSING EXECUTION TIMES

Table F-19 indicates the number of clock periods for exception processing. The number of clock periods includes the time for all stacking, the vector fetch, and the fetch of the first two instruction words of the handler routine. The number of bus read and write cycles is shown in parenthesis as (r/w).

Table F-19. Exception Processing Execution Times

Exception	
Address Error	126(4/26)
Breakpoint Instruction*	42(5/4)
Bus Error	126(4/26)
CHK Instruction**	44(5/4) +
Divide By Zero	42(5/4)
Illegal Instruction	38(4/4)
Interrupt*	46(5/4)
MOVEC, Illegal Cr**	46(5/4)
Privilege Violation	38(4/4)
Reset***	40(6/0)
RTE, Illegal Format	50(7/4)
RTE, Illegal Revision	70(12/4)
Trace	38(4/4)
TRAP Instruction	38(4/4)
TRAPV Instruction	40(5/4)

+ add effective address calculation time.
  *The interrupt acknowledge and breakpoint cycles are assumed to take four clock periods.
  **Indicates maximum value.
  ***Indicates the time from when $\overline{RESET}$ and $\overline{HALT}$ are first sampled as negated to when instruction execution starts.

APPENDIX G
MC68010 LOOP MODE OPERATION

The MC68010 has several features that provide efficient execution of program loops. One of these features is the DBcc looping primitive instruction. The DBcc instruction operates on three operands, a loop counter, a branch condition, and a branch displacement. When the DBcc is executed in loop mode, the contents of the low order word of the register specified as the loop counter is decremented by one and compared to minus one. If equal to minus one, the result of the decrement is placed back into the count register and the next sequential instruction is executed, otherwise the condition code register is checked against the specified branch condition. If the condition is true, the result of the decrement is discarded and the next sequential instruction is executed. Finally, if the count register is not equal to minus one and the branch condition is false, the branch displacement is added to the program counter and instruction execution continues at that new address. Note that this is slightly different than non-looped execution; however, the results are the same.

An example of using the DBcc instruction in a simple loop for moving a block of data is shown in Figure G-1. In this program, the block of data 'LENGTH' words long at address 'SOURCE' is to be moved to address 'DEST' provided that none of the words moved are equal to zero. When the effect of instruction prefetch on this loop is examined it can be seen that the bus activity during the loop execution would be:

1. Fetch the MOVE.W instruction,
2. Fetch the DBEQ instruction,
3. Read the operand where A0 points,
4. Write the operand where A1 points,
5. Fetch the DBEQ branch displacement, and
6. If loop conditions are met, return to step 1.

```
          LEA      SOURCE, A0      Load A Pointer To Source Data
          LEA      DEST, A1        Load A Pointer To Destination
          MOVE.W   #LENGTH, D0     Load The Counter Register
LOOP      MOVE.W   (A0) + , (A1) + Loop To Move The Block Of Data
          DBEQ     D0, LOOP        Stop If Data Word Is Zero
```

Figure G-1. DBcc Loop Program Example

During this loop, five bus cycles are executed; however, only two bus cycles perform the data movement. Since the MC68010 has a two word prefetch queue in addition to a one word instruction decode register, it is evident that the three instruction fetches in this loop could be eliminated by placing the MOVE.W word in the instruction decode register and holding the DBEQ instruction and its branch displacement in the prefetch queue. The MC68010 has the ability to do this by entering the loop mode of operation. During loop mode operation, all opcode fetches are suppressed and only operand reads and writes are performed until an exit loop condition is met.

MC68010

Loop mode operation is transparent to the programmer, with only two conditions required for the MC68010 to enter the loop mode. First, a DBcc instruction must be executed with both branch conditions met and a branch displacement of minus four; which indicates that the branch is to a one word instruction preceding the DBcc instruction. Second, when the processor fetches the instruction at the branch address, it is checked to determine whether it is one of the allowed looping instructions. If it is, the loop mode is entered. Thus, the single word looped instruction and the first word of the DBcc instruction will each be fetched twice when the loop is entered; but no instruction fetches will occur again until the DBcc loop conditions fail.

In addition to the normal termination conditions for a loop, there are several conditions that will cause the MC68010 to exit loop mode operation. These conditions are interrupts, trace exceptions, reset errors, and bus errors. Interrupts are honored after each execution of the DBcc instruction, but not after the execution of the looped instruction. If an interrupt exception occurs, loop mode operation is terminated and can be restarted on return from the interrupt handler. If the T bit is set, trace exceptions will occur at the end of both the loop instruction and the DBcc instruction and thus loop mode operation is not available. Reset will abort all processing, including the loop mode. Bus errors during the loop mode will be treated the same as in normal processing; however, when the RTE instruction is used to continue the execution of the looped instruction, the three word loop will not be re-fetched.

The loopable instructions available on the MC68010 are listed in Table G-1. These instructions may use the three address register indirect modes to form one word looping instructions; (An), (An) + , and − (An).

Table G-1. MC68010 Loopable Instructions

Opcodes	Applicable Addressing Modes		Opcodes	Applicable Addressing Modes
MOVE [BWL]	(Ay) to (Ax) − (Ay) to (Ax) (Ay) to (Ax) + − (Ay) to (Ax) + (Ay) to − (Ax) − (Ay) to − (Ax) (Ay) + to (Ax) Ry to (Ax) (Ay) + to (Ax) + Ry to (Ax) + (Ay) + to − (Ax)		ABCD [B] ADDX [BWL] SBCD [B] SUBX [BWL]	− (Ay) to − (Ax)
			CMP [BWL]	(Ay) + to (Ax) +
ADD [BWL] AND [BWL] CMP [BWL] OR [BWL] SUB [BWL]	(Ay) to Dx (Ay) + to Dx − (Ay) to Dx		CLR [BWL] NEG [BWL] NEGX [BWL] NOT [BWL] TST [BWL] NBCD [B]	(Ay) (Ay) + − (Ay)
ADDA [WL] CMPA [WL] SUBA [WL]	(Ay) to Ax − (Ay) to Ax (Ay) + to Ax		ASL [W] ASR [W] LSL [W]	(Ay) by #1 (Ay) + by #1 − (Ay) by #1
ADD [BWL] AND [BWL] EOR [BWL] OR [BWL] SUB [BWL]	Dx to (Ay) Dx to (Ay) + Dx to − (Ay)		LSR [W] ROL [W] ROR [W] ROXL [W] ROXR [W]	

NOTE
[B, W, or L] indicate an operand size of byte, word, or long word.

MC68010